# Reinforcement and Punishment:

## Vignettes for Practice in Applied Behavior Analysis

Joseph M. Strayhorn, Jr., M.D.

*Psychological Skills Press*

Wexford, Pennsylvania

Psychological Skills Press

263 Seasons Drive

Wexford, PA 15090

www.psychologicalskills.org

author's email: joestrayhorn@gmail.com

Cover photo is from shutterstock.com, photographed by "bikeriderlondon"


ISBN:  978-1-931773-20-1

# Contents

5

# The Goal of This Book

Why do we do what we do? To produce a consequence that we want, or to avoid one that we don't want. This statement oversimplifies, but it nevertheless powerfully helps us understand how behavior gets influenced for better or for worse.

We constantly do things, and our behaviors continually produce consequences. Those consequences teach us whether to repeat the behavior (or one like it) more often or less often. Consequences constantly give messages to our brains about the behaviors we've just done: "More often, please!" or "Less often, please!" Yet most people are not very tuned in to whether consequences are giving people's brains a "more often" or "less often" message.

This isn't a complete textbook on *applied behavior analysis* or *behavior modification*. Those two terms, which mean about the same thing, refer to the field that studies, among other things, how to bring out desirable behaviors by arranging the right consequences for them. I didn't try to teach the meanings of all the terms used in the field, nor to review the most important research, nor to examine the history of the field, even though I couldn't help mentioning some random bits of information in these areas. Rather, this book is meant to present lots of little stories that provide practice in thinking: "What behavior is being strengthened or weakened? What consequences do that?" Sometimes there's an additional question: "What consequences would do a better job of strengthening admirable behavior or reducing unwanted behavior?"

Some may say, "I don't subscribe to behaviorism," Or "I have a different orientation for thinking about people," Or "I think that applied behavior analysis oversimplifies human beings." I would never argue that reinforcement, non-reinforcement, and punishment form the whole story for understanding human behavior. And I would strongly debate certain parts of the philosophies of certain prominent behaviorists. But no matter what orientation or philosophy one endorses, a simple fact can't be denied: the consequences that result from any behavior tend to teach us whether to do that behavior more or less frequently in the future. No matter what philosophy I subscribe to, if someone gives my child very pleasant and desirable hugs and cookies every time he has a tantrum and hits, I'm in trouble.

I imagined as my audience parents and teachers who want to help children develop good habits. However, I believe the sort of thinking practiced here is useful for all who deal with human beings and/or animals.

## Three Types of Consequences for Two Types of Behaviors

A *reinforcer* is a consequence of a behavior that tends to *increase* the frequency of the behavior it follows. For example, each time someone does a job, the person gets money. As a result of this setup, the person does the job more frequently. From the fact that the person does the job more frequently, we infer that the money is a positive reinforcer. Reinforcing consequences give a "more often, please," message to the brain.

Sometimes consequences are reinforcing, even though they don't appear pleasant! Suppose that a child messes with things in the house that he's not permitted to touch (things like china cups, and we're imagining that these are not intrinsically very fun toys for this child.) Each time the child does this, a parent turns attention away from something else, or some other child, and commands, "Don't do that! Get away from that!" The child looks disappointed, but complies. But over time, the child goes to the forbidden objects more and more frequently. What do we infer from that? It appears that the commands of the parent were reinforcers for the child's handling the forbidden objects. In the short run, the parent's command terminated the behavior, but in the long run, the commands somehow told the brain, "Please do that more often!"

Reinforcers can be of two types: positive and negative. Positive reinforcement is delivering something desirable; negative reinforcement is turning off something undesirable. Negative reinforcement is different from punishment. Negative reinforcement increases the frequency of the behavior it follows, whereas punishment decreases it. Let's look at an example. Suppose bullies taunt me, but when I pull out a weapon, their taunts cease and they leave me. The threat from the weapon punished their taunts, and reduced their frequency to zero, at least for a while. So the taunting behavior was punished by the weapon-displaying consequence. On the other hand, my brain has received a "more often, please," message, because my behavior achieved a desirable result. I have been (negatively) reinforced for pulling out the weapon by the desirable consequence of the cessation of taunting. Thus I'm more likely to pull the weapon next time. I have been negatively reinforced for punishing them! (My model has probably taught them to go and fetch weapons for themselves, but this is another story.)

Punishment is meant to reduce the frequency of a behavior by following it with consequences the person does not want. There are two types of punishment: the delivery of something unpleasant, or the withdrawal of something pleasant. The withdrawal of something pleasant is also called *response cost.* For example, when a child defies his parent, he loses the privilege of playing with an electronic game.

To give a response that is neither reinforcing nor punishing can be called "non-reinforcing" the behavior or "ignoring" the behavior.

Sometimes it's hard to decide whether to call a certain response to a behavior punishment or non-reinforcement. We're tend to feel punished when we fail to get a reinforcer that we strongly expected, or wished for, or felt we "deserved." If I were told, "You're not getting a paycheck for the last month's work," I would probably feel more strongly punished than if someone had slapped my hand with a ruler, even though all that's happening is that I'm not getting an expected reinforcer. Suppose a child has a temper tantrum (screaming, crying, saying very angry words...) The child expects, from past experience, that parents will give constant attention, attempt to soothe, try to figure out what the child needs and supply it. If the child is made to go to a time out room and stay there alone for a while, that's punishment. But what if the parents simply do nothing – go about their business, work in the house, attend to other family members, not look at or speak to the child? We'll call this "non-reinforcement" or ignoring. But because the child expected reinforcement instead, the child may experience inattention as the withdrawal of a reinforcer, which we earlier defined as response cost, a type of punishment. But it's so different from actively doing something unpleasant to the child that it gets a different name.

If we get lots less than we expect, we feel punished; if we get at least as much as we expect, we feel rewarded. (John Watson and other early theorists called "methodological behaviorists" wanted to eliminate from the science of behavior any internal states such as thoughts, feelings, and expectations. But this strategy appears quite inefficient. People can tell us about their thoughts and expectations, and hearing these reports can be quite useful!)

Thus consequences can be either reinforcing, punishing, or non-reinforcing. And there's nothing else left for them to be! For that reason, the consequences of our actions constantly give us the "more often!" or "less often!" feedback. When we are with anyone, everything we do must be either reinforcing, punishing, or non-reinforcing. People constantly influence each other through the consequences they furnish. As thousands or millions of consequences accumulate, people can affect each other's habits dramatically.

For brevity, I made up some acronyms: RAB, RUB, NAB, NUB, PAB, and PUB. The R, N, and P stand for reinforcement, non-reinforcement, and punishment. The AB and UB stand for admirable behavior and unwanted behavior.

To be a good influence, we want to reinforce admirable behavior. Let's call "reinforcing admirable behavior" RAB. We don't want to reinforce unwanted behavior. Let's call "reinforcing unwanted behavior" RUB. Let's call "non-reinforcing unwanted behavior" NUB, and "non-reinforcing admirable behavior" NAB. Similarly, punishing admirable and unwanted behavior are PAB and PUB, respectively. Thus we have 3 types of consequences (reinforcement, non-reinforcement, and punishment) and 2 types of behavior (admirable and unwanted) and thus we have 6 different combinations.

Let's think about these one by one. RAB is almost always a good thing. But sometimes what we think reinforces admirable behavior may even punish it. For example: a child is playing with a friend. The parent occasionally comes and pats her child on the back and says, "You're playing so nicely with your friend; I'm proud of you." But this particular child happens to find this praise very embarrassing. It happens to be punishment instead of reinforcement.

Identifying RAB is complicated in another way: people can disagree on what is admirable behavior. For example, winning boxing matches or mixed martial arts contests is viewed by many as highly admirable; in the value systems of nonviolence advocates (including myself), such violent behavior is highly unwanted.

RUB, or reinforcing unwanted behavior, is responsible for lots of undesirable behavior, and thence a lot of human misery. But it's very difficult to avoid it altogether. For example, often our attention is reinforcing, but often we can't help but attend to unwanted behavior in order to put a stop to it.

NAB, or non-reinforcing admirable behavior, one may think, is a bad thing – whenever something admirable occurs, it should be reinforced. But it's impossible to reinforce every single admirable behavior externally. People need to learn to do admirable things without someone's giving them a pat on the back or a prize every time they do so. Sometimes it's good to provide *intermittent reinforcement*, where reinforcement comes after admirable behavior only a certain fraction of the time, and unpredictably. Sometimes an expert teacher will purposely start off by reinforcing the desired behavior every time it occurs – this is called *continuous reinforcement*. Once the behavior is occurring frequently, the teacher gradually makes the schedule of reinforcement "leaner." The behavior becomes reinforced about half the times it occurs,  then maybe one third of the times,  and thence less and less. Perhaps eventually the behavior is only reinforced once in hundreds of trials. When the behavior is called "work," the result of progressively getting used to a leaner reinforcement schedule has been called (by psychologist Robert Eisenberger) *learned industriousness*. Gradually getting used to doing more and more work before the reinforcer helps the person be more persistent, and less dependent on external reinforcement. (Landmark work on the timing of reinforcement, as well as much other work on other aspects of reinforcement, was done by B.F. Skinner.)

So NAB can help build persistence, but usually only when the person already does the behavior fairly often. When you are trying to first get the behavior into the person's repertoire, NAB usually represents a missed opportunity.

NUB is often sufficient to eliminate an undesirable behavior, particularly when it replaces

RUB. If possible, we want to reduce unwanted behavior by just ignoring it or non-reinforcing it, or taking away whatever reinforcing consequences currently exist. But our NUB doesn't work when there's some RUB that we don't take away. For example, it doesn't work when a teacher ignores a bully's extortion of desirable things from peers.

PAB, or punishing admirable behavior, is something a behavior modifier almost never seeks to arrange. But the world doles out PAB and it's good for people to experience some of it, in order to learn to handle it. I play my best in a tennis tournament, and lose. I work hard on an article, submit it, and receive a humiliating rejection. I am kind to someone, and the person acts rude and entitled in response. Although it's fortunately not true that "No good deed goes unpunished," many good deeds are punished. Building up some resistance to PAB may help people become resilient and resistant to demoralization. This resilience especially comes when PAB is eventually followed by RAB: the person works hard and fails, then works much more and succeeds. Psychotherapists often try to help people to get the successes that break the string of failures, the RAB that ends the string of PABs. In retrospect, the PABs may be seen as useful in building resilience. But without the RAB, an unbroken string of PABs tends to demoralize almost everyone sooner or later.

PUB, the punishing of unwanted behavior, seems to be, for many people, the default method of influencing others. This default strategy seems to be: "If people are doing what we want, there's no need to do anything; if they do what we don't want, zap them for it." But PUB often leads to vicious cycles. From the other person's point of view, the punishment that I deliver is unwanted behavior, and the other person likely gets the urge to punish me back for it. This unwanted punishment from the other in turn may spur me to punish back even more severely. The escalation of PUB in response to PUB is responsible for much violence.

There's another problem with PUB: it often results in a behavior's being done on the sly rather than being eliminated or reduced. Children who are punished for getting junk food without permission often learn to sneak and get the junk food when no one is looking. Successfully avoiding PUB through lying or stealing turns the result into RUB – escape from punishment reinforces dishonesty.

There are other problems with PUB. When someone delivers a certain amount of PUB, the recipient may become angry or even hateful toward the punisher. The recipient can form the goal of frustrating and not pleasing the punisher. As a result, the praise and approval that the punisher later gives can become no longer reinforcing, or even punishing. In other words, PUB can decrease our power to give RAB.

Here's another problem with PUB: Society has an interest in suppressing "vigilante justice" and thus imposes limits on the extent to which one person is permitted to punish another, before the vigilante gets punished by law enforcers.

Finally, punishing unwanted behavior may also punish admirable behavior. For example, an adolescent gets so frequently punished for not paying attention in class that the adolescent drops out of school altogether. Someone tried to punish "inattention" but ended up punishing "showing up at school."

Despite all these complications, sometimes PUB is the only strategy that works to eliminate or reduce an unwanted behavior.

| RAB | Reinforcing Admirable Behavior | Almost always good to do |
|-----|--------------------------------|--------------------------|
| RUB | Reinforcing Unwanted Behavior | Almost always not a good plan |
| NAB | Non-reinforcing Admirable Behavior | Can't fully avoid it; sometimes used on purpose to build persistence |
| NUB | Non-reinforcing Unwanted Behavior | Works if you take away all the reinforcers that sustain the behavior |
| PAB | Punishing Admirable Behavior | Avoid doing it on purpose. But can sometimes build resilience. |
| PUB | Punishing Unwanted Behavior | It's complicated. |

Most people go through life hardly aware of which of these they are doing at any given moment. Many, or perhaps most, people do lots of accidental RUB with others. Our goal is to become very aware of how consequences affect behavior. We'll look at lots of examples. Each vignette will ask you to analyze what is going on. Are consequences providing a good or bad influence? What behavior is being strengthened or weakened? How could consequences be used better? After deciding these things for yourself, you can compare your analysis with mine.

People often evaluate whether their strategies "work" or not by observing only very short-term consequences. I hugged the child, and he stopped tantrumming; therefore, I may think, my strategy "worked." We paid the kidnappers ransom, and they returned the hostage; everything came out fine. When a child was hitting people, we figured out what he wanted and gave it to him; he stopped hitting; thus giving in was a successful strategy. But here's the fundamental question: *What did our response do to the probability that the behavior (e.g. tantrumming, kidnapping, hitting) will recur, after this episode is over?* Usually we can only know the answer to this for certain if the consequence is given repeatedly and we notice the frequency of the behavior over time. But even asking the fundamental question sometimes leads us to a pretty good hunch. If someone gets something very desirable as a consequence for a behavior, we can expect the probability of recurrence to go up.

The point of this book is to practice asking this fundamental question. Here it is in other words: "How did the consequence affect the probability of future recurrence of the behavior?" Or in still other words: "What behavior was reinforced, punished, or non-reinforced?"

Parents, families, classrooms, workplaces, nations, and humanity as a whole desperately need more admirable behavior. We need productive work toward worthy goals, kindness and respect, peaceful conflict-resolution, joyous socialization, careful good decisions, health and safety promoting actions, and intellectual curiosity. We just as desperately need less unwanted behavior: less violence, drug and alcohol abuse, self-injurious behavior, hostility, exploitation, paralysis by fear, demoralization, time-wasting.... It is by no means easy to arrange consequences that will strengthen the admirable behaviors and weaken the unwanted ones. But thinking about how consequences can best bring out admirable behavior is a very important step toward happier and more successful children, happier families, productive and joyous classrooms and workplaces, and a better society.

## The Vignettes

## 1. Parent reinforces tantrums in checkout line.

A child is with his parent at the grocery store. In the checkout line, the child demands that the parent buy him a candy bar. The parent says no. The child begins to scream louder and louder. Finally the parent, embarrassed, says, "Oh, all right, but you've got to quiet down!" The parent picks up the candy bar the child wants and buys it.

Analysis: This is a classical example of RUB: reinforcing unwanted behavior. The parent's "giving in" and agreeing to get the candy bar is the reinforcer. It's a "secondary reinforcer," because it signals that the candy bar, a "primary reinforcer," is coming.

## 2. Child reinforces parent's giving in, in checkout line.

To continue: when the parent gives in, the child stops screaming. The parent experiences great relief. Because of this, the parent is a little more likely to give in, in the future, and use RUB with the child more often.

Analysis: The stopping of the screaming is a very desirable event for the parent, and a big reward, even though it is the cessation of something negative rather than the onset of something positive. For this reason it's called a *negative reinforcer.* It reinforces the parent for giving in to the child's unreasonable demands. Thus the child is reinforcing "giving in" behavior in the parent. Since the parent's behavior is not good for either the child or the parent, the child's reinforcement of it is RUB. Both parent and child are using RUB with each other.

## 3. Checkout line part 3: Intermittent reinforcement produces stronger habits.

Two parents have the "tantrums in the checkout line" problem with their children. The first parent gives in immediately, at the very first sign that the child is starting to get upset. The second parent is a little more enlightened about reinforcement, and tries very hard not to reinforce the tantrums. The second parent at times waits until the child is screaming very loudly, and then gives in. Then the second parent gets even more determined, and refuses to give in much of the time, but still gives in about a quarter of the time.

Then both parents finally become convinced to completely stop reinforcing the tantrum behavior in stores. The first parent finds that the tantrums cease quickly. The second parent finds that it takes many more trials before the child finally ceases to tantrum.

Analysis: This vignette is meant to illustrate an important point: *intermittent reinforcement builds resistance to extinction. Intermittent reinforcement* means, for example, giving the child what he wants about every fourth time he tries for it, unpredictably, rather than every time. *Continuous reinforcement*, by contrast, means that the behavior gets rewarded every time. *Extinction* of a response means the gradual disappearance of a behavior when it ceases to get reinforced.

Why is an intermittently reinforced behavior more resistant to extinction? Because the person has learned to persist even when reinforcement doesn't come immediately. The person has learned, "Just because I didn't get what I wanted this time, I won't give up, because I still may get it the next time." For an admirable behavior, that persistence is good, and for unwanted behavior, it's bad! Thus, if what is being reinforced is unwanted behavior, the intermittent reinforcement puts the parent in a worse situation than if they'd reinforced it each time.

To build lasting desirable habits most efficiently, you use continuous reinforcement at the beginning, to get the frequency of the behavior high, and then you start making the reinforcement more intermittent, moving toward a "leaner" schedule of reinforcement, so that the behavior is more resistant to extinction. But this is exactly what you *don't* want to do with unwanted behaviors!

An important lesson: if you are going to stop reinforcing an unwanted behavior, stop completely! Otherwise, you are using intermittent reinforcement that builds habits that are harder to break.

Parents are punished enough by children's tantrums in stores that the option they often choose is not extinction, but going to the store without the child, if there is someone else to take care of him or her. In the following vignette, a parent tries still another strategy.

## 4. Checkout line part 4. Candy to reinforce cooperation rather than tantrums.

A parent buys several candy pieces. Before the parent and the child go into the store, the parent shows the child a piece of candy and says, "This is going to be the reward for good store behavior.

Good store behavior means that you do everything I ask you to do, right away. It also means that you use your inside voice the whole time. We can chat while we're in the store. I don't want you to even ask me to buy you anything. If you do, the answer will be no. If you whine or scream or keep asking me, that is not good store behavior. As soon as we get back to the car, you get the candy if you've had good store behavior the whole time."

Analysis: Now the parent is using the same reinforcer that would have reinforced tantrums, to reinforce their opposite. The offer of candy is made at a time where the child is not misbehaving, and this makes a huge difference.

Does using a certain food as a reinforcer make it even more desirable than it would otherwise be? Are there other harms from using junk food as contingent reinforcement? My guess is that using small quantities of junk food as reinforcement for positive behavior is a skill that is quite useful even for adults, and that childhood experiences of such contingent reinforcement do more good than harm, if done properly.

## 5. Siblings arguing.

Two siblings argue with each other in a disrespectful way. When they do so, the parent

comes near them and says, "You two stop arguing."
But over time, the frequency of hostile words goes
up and up.

The parent, noticing this, decides to ignore
the arguing and to watch for episodes when they are
friendly and cooperative with each other. Upon
seeing these episodes, the parent goes over and pats
the children on the back and observes and maybe
comments on what they're doing, in a way that
doesn't distract them from their fun. The frequency
of hostile words goes down and the frequency of
pleasant words goes up.

Analysis: At first, there was RUB. The parent
was wise enough to see that the command to stop
arguing, and the attention that came with it, were
probably reinforcing, because the unwanted
behavior became more frequent. The parent, upon
realizing this, shifted to NUB and RAB – the
unwanted behavior was non-reinforced and the
admirable behavior was reinforced. The changes in
frequency of the behaviors confirmed the parent's
hypothesis that parental attention was an important
reinforcer.

## 6. Off task at school gets back rub.

A child at school gets off task and doesn't

focus on his schoolwork. When this happens, his teacher rubs his back. This seems to help him in the short run to get back on task. But over time, he gets distracted more and more often.

Analysis: This is classic RUB, as well as being a back rub. The teacher, with such pleasant reinforcement, is teaching the child to get off task more often. Nurturing people often tend to rub and stroke people with whom they sympathize. But when unwanted behavior evokes that sympathy, rubs are often RUB.

## 7. New deal with back rubs at school.

The teacher in the previous story decides to try something different. When the child is off task, she rubs the back of some other child who is working well. Only the child is working well does she come and rub his back. She notices this distracts him a little in the short run, but over time, he starts to focus on his work more frequently.

Analysis: Now the teacher has moved from RUB to NUB and RAB – she's now non-reinforcing the unwanted behavior, and reinforcing the admirable behavior. Systematically reinforcing a certain type of behavior and not reinforcing another is called "differential reinforcement." At first, the teacher was using "differential reinforcement" in the wrong direction; upon switching to NUB and RAB, she used it in the right direction. In both cases, she noticed that the short term effects of her interventions were in the opposite direction from the longer term effects!

## 8. Disruption at preschool summons mom.

A child is at preschool. She doesn't like separating from her mother. When she gets really disruptive – knocking things over, refusing to comply, throwing things – the consequence is that the teachers call her mother to come and either take her home, or just help her calm down. She calms down and is happy upon seeing her mother. This gives everyone the impression that the mother's intervention is a good thing to do, a useful way of ending disruptive behavior. But the disruptive behavior gets more and more frequent.

Analysis: This is another classic RUB. The parent's appearance is a very powerful reinforcer. It follows the disruptive behavior, and reinforces it.

## 9. New deal for disruption at preschool.

To continue the previous story, a consultant recommends that the mother be called to come to see the child when the child has been respectful and cooperative for a while (with the length of time gradually increasing). When the child gets disruptive, the staff members try to tend to the other children and make their experiences as protected and positive as possible. The frequency of the child's disruptive behavior plummets.

Analysis: Now there is a change from RUB to RAB and NUB. When the admirable behavior is reinforced and the unwanted behavior is non-reinforced, the child's behavior improves.

## 10. It's just conversation... plus differential reinforcement.

A tutor works with a child daily. Part of their session is spent just chatting with one another. Anger control and not-fighting are important goals for the child.

When the child mentions wanting to beat someone up, or playing a violent video game, or someone's getting revenge on someone else, or calling someone a name, the tutor listens well, but with slow speech and a somber tone. When the child mentions doing something kind for someone, persuading people not to fight, helping out a younger child, wanting to stop wars, and so forth, the tutor responds in a super-animated way. Over a long time of tutoring, the parent observes that the child seems to get into fewer fights and to develop much better anger control.

Analysis: The tutor's tone of voice fails to reinforce a fascination with violence and anger, or at least does not reinforce it very much – relatively speaking, there is NUB. The tutor's voice greatly reinforces the expression of values of kindness and nonviolence – there is RAB in response to this.

When someone systematically reinforces one class of behavior much more than another class, we say that *differential reinforcement* is taking place. Differential reinforcement can be either deliberate or inadvertent. The combination of NUB and RAB is differential reinforcement in the right direction; the combination of NAB and RUB is differential reinforcement in the wrong direction!

It's a little startling to realize that it's almost impossible to have a conversation without both giving and receiving differential reinforcement. Both we and the persons we talk with almost always respond in ways that are at least a little more pleasant to some utterances than to others. The way we speak to others is influenced by countless hours of differential reinforcement we've experienced.

## 11. Showing off the A to dad, take 1.

A little girl runs up to her dad and says, "Look what I did! I got an A on the test!" The dad notices that it's past bedtime and replies, "You should have been in bed 20 minutes ago. Get upstairs and get ready for bed, NOW!"

Analysis: The child has done at least two admirable behaviors: doing well on the test (a productivity celebration) and feeling good about her accomplishment (a joyousness celebration). The lack of any attention to her performance on the test or her celebration of it is NAB (non-reinforcing admirable behavior), and the harsh tones in the command to get ready for bed constitute PAB (punishing admirable behavior).

## 12. Showing off the A to dad, take 2.

A different girl runs up to her dad and says, "Look what I did! I got an A on the test!" The dad looks at the paper wide-eyed, hugs his daughter and says, "Congrats to you, A-getter! You did good work!" He looks over the paper with the child for a while, commenting favorably on the various answers the child gave. Then he notices that it's 20 minutes past bedtime. He says, "Oh my gosh, it's past bedtime. Let's go see how fast we can get ready! I'll run up with the A-getter!" The girl laughs and runs upstairs with her dad, and the dad exclaims, "Such a fast-running A-getter! Getting to the toothbrush fast!" The girl giggles at this.

Analysis: In this example we have two RABs: reinforcement for getting the good grade and for celebrating it with the dad, and then reinforcement for the swift actions to get ready for bed.

## 13. Curious about space travel.

A child asks, "Has anyone ever traveled in a rocket ship to the sun?" The parent says, in a disapproving tone, "At your age, you should know better than that. Of course not. The sun would vaporize them." An older brother overhears this and keeps teasing the child for days afterward, saying things like, "Ready for your trip to the sun? Got your sun screen lotion yet?" "I have something for you – it's a little fan to keep cool with on your trip to the sun!"

Analysis: It's admirable that the child conjures up an interest in learning something. That behavior is punished by the solemn disapproval of the parent, and probably even more punished by the gleeful but sadistically bullying derision of the older brother. There's a big dose of PAB that may make the child think twice about being curious in the presence of his family members ever again.

## 14. Argumentative car ride.

Riding in the car, the child makes several attempts at conversation, but the parent is thinking about something else and doesn't reply.

The parent then says to herself, "Next exit will get us to highway 281."

The child says, "You're wrong. That's not the right way to go at all."

Now the parent says, "What do you know about it? Have you been studying the map?"

The child says, "I sure have, and you haven't!"

The parent says, "What are you talking about? You haven't even held a map."

The child says, "I know what I'm talking about and you don't."

After a few episodes like this, the parent

notices that the argumentative behavior seems to be getting more frequent.

Analysis: The child's ordinary attempts at conversation are admirable behavior, which is non-reinforced: NAB. The child's unwanted argumentative behavior is reinforced by the animated involvement with and attention to the child: RUB. Someone objects: "The argumentative tones of the parent are unpleasant, and should be punishing rather than reinforcing." One of the most important principles of applied behavior analysis is that we decide whether something is reinforcing, not by guessing on the basis of what we ourselves would like or dislike, but by seeing whether the behavior becomes more or less frequent. In this case, since the behavior is becoming more frequent, and if we fail to come up with some other plausible reinforcer, we're forced to acknowledge that the parent's arguing is a net reinforcer, and not punishment.

## 15. Time out for hitting, version 1.

A child gets angry and fairly frequently hits family members. The family starts a custom where when the child hits, he must go to a room for two minutes; no one will interact with him during this time. If he refuses to go, he loses the privilege of playing with an electronic game for the next 24 hours. After doing this for a while, the family notices that the frequency of hitting goes down.

Analysis: There are two PUBs: punishing the hitting with the time out, and punishing any refusal to go to time out with the loss of the privilege. In this case PUB worked.

## 16. Time out for hitting, version 2.

A child hits family members. The family demands that he go to time out each time he hits. When he refuses to go to time out, the family members argue with him, plead with him, sometimes physically try to drag him, or yell at him. The family notices that the frequency of hitting is going up rather than down.

Analysis: What the parents hoped would be PUB appears to be RUB. That is, the high-stimulation arguing and wrestling and being pleaded with appear to be positive reinforcement rather than punishment for this child. Very often children would rather have attention and stimulation, even of a negative sort, than inattention, and excited verbalizations (even though they're angry) are positive reinforcers.

## 17. Ignoring the stealing.

A child at school steals food from the other children. The teacher decides to ignore this behavior, and see if the ignoring reduces its frequency. When the child sees that he can get away with stealing, he steals more often.

Analysis: The teacher's idea is to use NUB, non-reinforcement of unwanted behavior. The problem is that the unwanted behavior is reinforced by the food itself. The fact that the student doesn't get the teacher's attention for this doesn't reduce the behavior, because the teacher's attention isn't the behavior the student is after – it's the food. So the whole setup is RUB.

## 18. Disruption at school, ended by counselor – for now.

A child at school flies off the handle at times and knocks things around the room. The guidance counselor theorizes that the child is in need of a certain type of sensory stimulation, and that a hug will provide the right sort of sensory input. The counselor comes in and hugs the child during these episodes, and miraculously the hugs seem to bring each episode to an end. But over time, the episodes become more and more frequent.

Analysis: Hugs are very often reinforcing, and in this case, they are contingent upon unwanted behavior. This is classic RUB. Here's a sentence for us to meditate upon: Stimuli which 'work' to end an episode of unwanted behavior can nonetheless also 'work' to make those episodes occur more often! Or: What terminates a behavior can also reinforce it.

## 19. The words must have good music.

Two parents try watching for the positive examples of psychological skills that their children do, and reinforcing them immediately afterward with approval.

The first parent says things like, "Oh, I like that. That was a good example of fortitude. How did you get the fortitude to do that?"

The second parent says exactly the same sorts of words!

The second parent notices a big increase in positive examples over time, and the first parent notices a much smaller response.

A specialist listens to each of them. The first parent speaks in a subdued, quiet, monotone voice.

The second parent speaks in a voice with great variation in pitch, volume, and tempo. The second's utterances sound really excited, whereas the first's sound somewhat depressed.

Analysis: What makes approval reinforcing? For most children, the tones of voice are more important than the semantic content of the words. When songwriters want to stir up positive emotion, they use faster tempo, greater pitch variation, and a louder volume. For most children, these elements are important, and the most important of them, in my estimation, is pitch variation – not being monotone.

## 20. "Sounding and blending" each day.

For 5 or 10 minutes a day, the child works with a tutor on "sounding and blending" words in word lists. (Sounding and blending means saying the individual sounds and then blending them together to say the word.) As the student does this, the tutor exclaims, "Good!" or "Yes!" or "You got it!" after each word, and clicks a tally counter. At the end of the activity the tutor exuberantly reports how many points the student has gotten. When the cumulative point total reaches certain round numbers, the student receives a certificate and a prize.

Analysis: Classic RAB. The exclamations of approval are called "social reinforcers," and the prizes are "tangible reinforcers." The points are "secondary reinforcers," because they are associated with getting the prizes. The child's being willing to comply with this activity, which is hard work but very useful in increasing reading skill, is admirable indeed. The child is learning not just reading skills, which are hugely important, but also compliance and self-discipline skills, which are even more so.

## 21. Hard work by child, but little payoff.

A child works extremely hard on schoolwork and athletics. But the child's talent is such that there is mediocre achievement in both areas. The child is very loving and conscientious in taking care of her pet; no humans acknowledge this. When the parent sees that the child's room is messy, the parent withdraws a privilege, and when the child is defiant and hostile, the parent ignores these verbalizations.

Analysis: The child is existing largely under conditions of NAB – the admirable productivity in

47

academics and athletics and pet care goes non-reinforced (except perhaps by the pet's RAB). The parent uses PUB for the non-cleaning of the room, and NUB for the hostility. It's good that the parent didn't reinforce the hostility. But what this child probably needs for happiness is a lot more RAB. A very important ingredient for happiness is the "effort-payoff connection": the sense that your efforts at least have a chance to pay off in getting you what you want.

Many authorities on education would like to deny that some children can work very hard and still not excel at academic skills (with excelling defined as age- or grade-standardized test performance.) The idea that if expectations are high, children will meet them, can do much harm. The sad fact is that some children work hard enough but still don't learn what most age-mates do. To work hard for the payoff of being told "You passed, but just barely" is a condition under which only the most resilient personalities can maintain morale; when the message invariably is "You failed," the task of maintaining morale becomes almost impossible. Reinforcing movements up a hierarchy of difficulty, wherever the child is starting from, even if the movements are small, is part of the answer. Reinforcing non-academic work in addition to academic work is often another part of the answer.

## 22. Sullen at the party.

A child goes to a party with the parent. She looks sullen and refuses to speak to anybody. The parent asks her why she doesn't want to speak, and repeatedly urges and then commands her to play with someone. The child refuses, defiantly. The parent says, "If you'll play with someone, I'll buy you a toy on the way home." The child still refuses, for the time being.

Analysis: The *offer* for a new toy is a reinforcer, and the repeated urgings of the parent are probably more reinforcing than punishing. The child finds out that by refusing to interact and by refusing to comply with the parent, this behavior gives her power. Ceasing the withdrawn behavior is a bargaining chip that the child can exchange for a toy. Thus the offer of the toy reinforces the unwanted behavior, and we are in classic RUB territory.

## 23. Punished for misdeeds reported by sibling.

A child's sister reports to the parents the bad behaviors the child does; the parents withdraw privileges for those behaviors. The child learns to do the behaviors whenever there is no chance of getting caught. In addition, the child reports hating the sister.

Analysis: This vignette illustrates why PUB is complicated. It can result in resourceful efforts at deception (which are in a sense reinforced by the absence of punishment, contrasting with the punishment that occurs without the deception.) It can also induce powerful negative emotional responses.

## 24. Multiple commands, the last of which gets (sometimes) obeyed.

A child is playing a video game. A parent tells the child to turn it off; the child ignores the command. The parent repeats the command 8 times. Finally, the child finishes up the game. Something similar happens when the parent asks the child to come along for an appointment, brush teeth, go to bed, come in from outside, come to supper, help with a chore, and so forth. Over time, the child more and more frequently ignores the parent's commands.

Analysis: The child is reinforced for ignoring the command by getting to keep doing what the child was doing – for example, getting to continue playing the video game is a consequence that reinforces ignoring the parent's commands. If the parent gives 9 commands and only the last one is obeyed, the child is getting 8 times more practice in noncompliance than in compliance. And since this is reinforced practice, lots of RUB is going on.

For this reason some advise parents to give a command only once, and then follow through with "physical guidance" to enforce the command (for example, after the command, "It's time for us to go now," is ignored, the parent takes the child by the hand and starts walking.)  Or if physical guidance is not possible, the first noncomply is followed by a consequence (such as a time out or withdrawal of a privilege). In this case the noncompliance results in PUB. If the parent figures out a way to reinforce compliance on the "first ask," for example by attention and approval, that is RAB.

## 25. Convicted by confession.

Two children hit other children. The authorities ask, "Did you hit?" One child confesses and is punished. The other lies, denies hitting, and escapes punishment.

Analysis: For the first child, there is PUB for

the hitting, but there is PAB for the admirable behavior of being honest. Probably the first child is learning, "Next time I'll lie." For the second child, there is NUB delivered by the authorities, but probably RUB delivered in the form of power over others, for the hitting. The second child gets RUB for the behavior of lying – the reinforcement is escape from the expected punishment.

## 26. "Sit down" and out-of-seat behavior.

Children are doing independent work in a classroom. The teacher adopts a new policy: Each time a child gets out of his or her seat, the teacher "redirects" the child by asking the child to sit down and get back to work. The child almost always obeys. Thus it appears that the redirection "works" in promoting sitting. But as time goes by, the children get out of their seats more and more frequently. Then the teacher drops this policy. The frequency of out-of-seat behavior falls. She reenacts the policy. The frequency of out-of-seat behavior rises again. Then the teacher enacts a new policy: the teacher completely ignores out-of-seat behavior and pays attention only to the most productive children. The rate of out-of-seat behavior falls to the lowest levels that it has ever been.

Analysis: From the fact that the frequency of out-of-seat behavior rose when the teacher adopted the redirection policy, we infer that redirection reinforced the behavior of getting out of seat, even though it prompted the behavior of getting back into seat. So there was RUB going on. When the teacher changed to ignoring the out-of-seat behavior and attending to the productive children, now there was a combination of NUB (non-reinforcing the unwanted out-of-seat behavior) and RAB (reinforcing the admirable behavior of working). The combination of NUB and RAB means that "differential reinforcement" is working in the right direction.

This vignette is lifted from a study recounted in *Parents Are Teachers* by Wesley Becker.

## 27. Paying the audience to put phones away.

This is a fanciful example.

A very wealthy speaker who doesn't know much about applied behavior analysis has a strong aversion to audience members' looking at their cell phones. When he sees the first person look at the cell phone, he says, "I'll give you a hundred dollar bill if you'll put that cell phone away." The person puts the phone away, and the speaker comes through with the payment. Another person very soon after is found texting, and the speaker repeats the offer, which is gladly accepted. Within a very short time after implementing this plan, the speaker sees the entire audience busily texting.

Analysis: The imaginary speaker thought, "I'm reinforcing admirable behavior – putting away the cell phone and getting rid of the distraction." But the problem is that the behavior of "putting away the cell phone" is part of a "chain" of behavior: it necessitates the behavior of "starting to use the cell phone" in the first place. It's not possible to reinforce "putting it away" without also reinforcing "starting to use it."

For this reason, the speaker's reward is definitely RUB. He's spending money to get just the behavior he doesn't want!


## 28. Ransom to kidnappers.

Country A has a policy of never paying ransom to kidnappers. Country B often can be persuaded to pay large ransom for the release of hostages when they are kidnapped. Over time, the citizens of Country B get kidnapped much more often.

Analysis: This is exactly analogous to our fanciful example with the speaker. When Country B reinforces the kidnappers for releasing the hostages, it is also reinforcing the part of the behavior chain that is necessary for releasing them, i.e. kidnapping them in the first place. Country A is using NUB and Country B is using RUB. (This doesn't guarantee that the leaders of Country A won't lose votes by being perceived as cruel and heartless.)

Those interested in American history may want to reread about the Barbary Pirate War, Thomas Jefferson, and the statement "Millions for defense, but not one cent for tribute."

## 29. Punishing the parent for response cost.

A parent decides to take away a privilege as a consequence for a child's misbehavior. The child has a fit and hits the parent and destroys things in the house. The parent concludes, "She doesn't respond well to punishment." The parent refrains from taking away privileges.

Analysis: The parents tried "response cost," which is withdrawing something reinforcing, as a consequence for misbehavior. This constitutes PUB.

But the child's fits punished the parent for using response cost. When the parent then canceled the response cost experiment, the cancellation is a reinforcer for the child. (Because it's the turning off of something negative rather than the turning on of something positive, it's called a negative reinforcer.) The child correctly infers that the cause of this reinforcer is her aggressive behavior. One of the main reasons for aggression is the power it conveys.

We often think that a reinforcer must immediately follow a behavior in order to be reinforcing. Sometimes this is true. But what is probably more important is that the person has a clear gut feeling that the behavior *causes* the reinforcer to come. Punishing unwanted behavior can be reinforced by the power it conveys, even if the payoff of reduced frequency of the unwanted behavior comes after some delay.

So the parent is attempting to use PUB, but the child uses PUB more powerfully. The parent's abandonment of the authoritative stance constitutes RUB – the parent is reinforcing the child's punishment, by being influenced by it.


## 30. Command without follow-up.

The parent gives the child a command, and then turns the attention elsewhere, without being able to see whether the child complied with the command or not.

Analysis: If the child complies, this is NAB. The parent misses out on an important opportunity for RAB, reinforcing the admirable behavior of complying by saying "Thank you," or whatever.

If, as is perhaps more likely, the child ignores the command, then the parent is using NUB, non-reinforcement of unwanted behavior. Why isn't this effective? Because the "unwanted behavior" of continuing to do whatever the child felt like doing is usually more pleasant than that of following the command. That is, the unwanted behavior is usually reinforced by something in the environment. The parent's NUB is outweighed by the environment's RUB. By giving the command and not following up on it, the parent let the environment reinforce noncompliance.

## 31. Time to go, but not really.

The parent and child are at a party. The parent says to the child, "Come on, it's time to go." But then the parent gets into a conversation with another parent for another 5 minutes.

Analysis: If the child obeys the parent by

stopping what she's doing and waiting by the parent's side, the child gets punished by having to wait through what is probably much less pleasant than what the child was doing before. In this case there is PAB, punishing the admirable behavior of the child.

On the other hand, if the child ignores the parent's command because this has happened several times before, the child gets to keep on in whatever reinforcing activity the child had chosen, rather than terminate it. The child is getting reinforced for the unwanted behavior of ignoring the parent's command. Now there is RUB in effect.

When the alternatives are PAB and RUB, it's good to employ an option that permits "neither of the above." What might this alternative be? How about: "It's time to go," followed by an immediate bee-line toward the exit door, followed by "Thanks for coming with me!"

## 32. Birthday satiation.

A child earns points for cooperation, chores, and high behavior ratings, that can be exchanged for Lego toys. This system seems to create not only better behavior, but more happiness in the child, as she has an effort-payoff connection – a sense that her efforts are getting something that she wants.

Then the child's birthday comes, and the child asks for Lego toys. The party guests compete with each other to see who can give the biggest and most expensive one. The grandparents, not to be outdone, supply even more.

Now the parents notice that the child's cooperation and willingness to do chores drop precipitously. The child says, "No thanks," and plays with Legos instead.

Analysis: There was a good system of RAB going on. But then it suddenly changed to NAB – the admirable behavior lost its reinforcer. Why? Because the child became "satiated" with the reinforcer. If you already have all you want of a reinforcer, getting more of it is not particularly pleasant. The child lost the "effort-payoff connection" once the payoffs were supplied in return for no effort. There must be some feeling of "deprivation" of a reinforcer in order for it to motivate us to do things.

The word *deprivation* sounds a little harsh. All I mean by it in this context is that in order for something to be reinforcing, you can't have already just had all you want of it!

Happiness in life is very closely linked to the effort-payoff connection. There must be some feeling of deprivation in order for payoffs to be appreciated. The interesting conclusion is that happiness results not from getting everything we want, but from wanting more than we have and feeling that our efforts are getting us what we want.

## 33. Values indoctrination.

Child A has been taught, for years, that making other people happy and making the world a better place are absolutely central to the good life. When the child does kind acts, the parent looks pleased, and talks about the child's kind acts, with approval, to the other parent. The child hears many stories of real and fictitious people's acts of kindness, with parents obviously greatly admiring those kind acts. The parents model kind acts frequently. The family repeats affirmations of the value of loving kindness. The parents greatly reinforce the child's reports of examples of kindness, either in the child's own behavior, other people's behavior, or observations of behavior the child collects.

Child B has been taught, for years, that winning competitions is key to the good life. Prevailing in verbal arguments, being dominant over other people, and being high on the pecking order are the supreme values that have gotten across to Child B.

In school, Child B locks another child in a locker. Other kids laugh. Child A gets the child out of the locker, despite the fact that other kids jeer at Child A.

Analysis: Learning values greatly influences what sort of situations are reinforcing or non-reinforcing or punishing for us. For Child B, the situation of "I am dominant over someone else" is highly reinforcing. For Child A, the event, "I have made someone happier" is highly reinforcing. Once those situations become powerful reinforcers, Child B experiences RUB for bullying behavior, while Child A experiences RAB for kind behavior.

Incidentally, in this vignette the bystanders to this bullying act, by their laughing and jeering, respectively, supplied some more RUB to the bully, and some PAB to the rescuer. They indicate that they too have internalized the value of dominance more than the value of kindness.

Behavior analysts speak of "establishing operations" as things that people do to make events reinforcing. Teaching the value of kindness makes the event of making someone else happy reinforcing. Teaching the value of dominance makes defeating someone else reinforcing.

A focus on the "establishing operations" of teaching values, in order to make certain outcomes become reinforcing, gets us away from the misperception or misapplication of behaviorism that seems to believe that the good society is to be achieved only by giving people an M&M candy each time they do something good!

## 34. Fred teaches Agnes to jump up the wall.

Fred is a psychologist, and Agnes is a Dalmatian dog. Fred's challenge is to quickly teach Agnes to face the wall and jump up. Some horizontal stripes are taped on the wall. Fred has a strobe light and some meat. Agnes is hungry.

First Agnes gets pretraining to learn that the light means, "Food is on the way!" This pretraining comes by flashing the light, and then giving Agnes a little food.

Then Fred carefully watches Agnes. When she happens to raise her head above the level of the lowest stripe, she gets a flash of light, followed by some food. After a little of this, the trainer "raises the bar," and Agnes gets the flash and the food only when her head goes about the next higher stripe, and then the next, and so forth. By about 20 minutes, she's jumping high up the wall.

Analysis: The flash of light in this case is called a *secondary reinforcer,* or one that becomes reinforcing because it's a signal that something already reinforcing (such as the meat) is coming. The meat is a *primary reinforcer.* Fred used the secondary reinforcer so that he could signal to Agnes the exact moment of her desirable behavior.

The reinforcement of successive approximations to the desired behavior (that is, Agnes's doing things that more and more closely resemble jumping up the wall) was named *shaping.* The artistry of the shaper is to be neither too stingy nor too indiscriminate with the reinforcement, but to apply it so as to most efficiently communicate to the shapee what to do.

Instead of a flash of light, animal trainers often use the sound of a clicker as a secondary reinforcer. If you search the Internet for "Clicker training," you will find many hits. Using the same basic procedure, animals who have needed uncomfortable veterinary procedures have been trained to accept these procedures without the need for anesthesia or physical coercion.

The coiner of the word shaping was B.F. Skinner, who was also "Fred" in the example above. The registered name of Agnes the Dalmatian was Roadcoach Cheerful. You can read about this historic shaping session in an article by Gail B.

Peterson, "The World's First Look At Shaping: B.F. Skinner's Gutsy Gamble," on the web at http://www.behavior.org/resources/478.pdf.

## 35. Disrespectful talk loses phone.

A child has spoken very disrespectfully to the parent. The parent lets the child know that the penalty for disrespectful talk will be the removal of the child's cell phone for a day. The parent also lets the child know ahead of time that the penalty for refusal to hand over the cell phone within an hour will be that the parent has the phone shut off through the phone company for one week. On the other hand, if the child does hand over the phone within an hour, the time that the phone is withheld will be reduced by a couple to a few hours.

The child speaks disrespectfully, and the parent demands the phone. In response, the child speaks even more disrespectfully, and the parent has the phone shut off for a week.

Analysis: The parent is obviously using the PUB strategy. This vignette illustrates that punishing unwanted behavior often elicits anger and even more unwanted behavior. When a parent plans to use PUB, it is usually necessary to make a plan in advance to deal with the unwanted behavior that the punishment elicits. Here the parent plans another PUB if the child refuses, and a RAB of reducing the penalty if the child cooperates in a timely manner.

What happens if the child punishes the parent for withdrawing the phone for a week, by stealing the parent's phone and hiding it? Or what if the child punishes the parent by putting ink on the parent's best clothes? The parent had best plan things carefully when using PUB; otherwise the one who is less ruthless and the one who is subject to child abuse laws may lose the power struggle.

## 36. Ignoring disrespectful talk.

The child is in the habit of speaking disrespectfully to the parent. The parent tries the strategy of ignoring the disrespectful utterances, and acting as if they had not occurred, and turning attention to household work or to another family member, while maintaining a "positive emotional climate" with the other family member. The parent finds this extremely difficult to do, but does it successfully. At first the rate of disrespectful utterances increases pretty dramatically. Then it gradually decreases over time, to a low level.

Analysis: The strategy here is NUB: non-reinforcing unwanted behavior. In fact, the turning of the attention away from the child to another family member may even constitute a mild form of PUB, if the loss of the parent's attention and interest is experienced as unpleasant. In this vignette the strategy worked. When the strategy works, it works because the reinforcer for the child's talk was the parent's offended reaction; when this reinforcer is withdrawn, the behavior decreases in frequency. Why is the parent's offended reaction sometimes reinforcing? Perhaps because it shows the child how much power he or she owns, to immediately control the emotional life of someone else.

When someone starts to use NUB, there is often a short-term increase in the rate of the behavior before it starts to decrease. The decrease in a behavior because of non-reinforcement is called *extinction*, and the short term increase is called an *extinction burst*. It's as if the person is saying, "Wait, it's not working? Let me try doing it faster and harder! ... Hmm, I guess it really doesn't work any more."

## 37. Fast and slow weight loss goals.

Two people go on weight-reducing diets. Person A shoots for very rapid weight loss, aiming to take in about 2000 calories fewer per day than are expended, and giving up of almost all the foods that are very reinforcing. Person B shoots for slower weight loss and smaller portions of reinforcing foods. Person A starts binging on junk food in moments of low self-discipline. Neither person is very successful at weight loss, but Person B does not develop binges.

Analysis: In this vignette I have neither person very successful at weight loss, to reflect the reality that weight loss is a goal for which "many are called and few are chosen." But the main thing this vignette illustrates is an earlier point that a reinforcer becomes more reinforcing, the more there is a state of deprivation for it. Person A created a strong deprivation state, which made junk food extremely reinforcing, and thus harder to resist. When the self-discipline reserves dropped below a certain threshold, binges resulted. The pleasure that high-caloric density food gives furnished RUB for both of them, but the RUB for person A was more intense than that for person B.

Of course, not everyone who shoots for rapid weight loss becomes a binge eater. There is tremendous variation among people. But as a general rule, the more extreme the deprivation, the higher likelihood of binging.

## 38. Missing the fortitude triumph.

A child has had a problem with having tantrums in stores when the parent refuses to buy her something. The child and the parent are at a store, and the child asks the parent to buy her something. The parent says, "No, we can't get that today." The child says nothing. The parent says nothing.

Analysis: The child's saying nothing was extremely admirable behavior relative to the customary behavior of having a tantrum. The parent's not reacting to this admirable behavior constitutes NAB. If the parent had said, "Good for you! I said no, and you handled it! That's a fortitude triumph for you!" then the parent would have used RAB. On the other hand, if the parent had said, "See, you've shown you can handle it when I say no. Now why didn't you do that before, instead of embarrassing me and throwing a tantrum?" – then the parent's reprimand for the past behavior, contingent on good behavior in the present, would have been punishing the admirable behavior – PAB.

## 39. Telling the therapist about the child's misbehavior.

A parent takes the child to a mental health professional. The child is not so sure he wants to do this, but he complies with the parent. The parent and child sit down in the office and the parent recites the bad behaviors the child has done, for a long time.

Analysis: The compliance of the child with the request to go to the appointment is punished by the consequence of having to sit and listen to a recitation of the bad behaviors – PAB. This is especially true if the default alternative was that the child would get to play video games instead. It is possible also that the fame and notice that the child gets for the bad behaviors that are recited may reinforce those behaviors – some RUB in addition to PAB. RUB and PAB are results that it would be good for an insurance company or a parent to pay NOT to get.

## 40. "May I have your attention, please?"

A parent is talking with another adult. The child comes up to the parent and waits. The parent goes on talking. The child quietly addresses the parent. The parent goes on talking. The child gets louder and louder and finally screams angrily at the parent. The parent turns to the child and says, "What!!"

Analysis: The parent first uses NAB, ignoring the admirable behavior, and then reinforces the unwanted form of attention-getting. First NAB and then RUB constitutes "differential reinforcement" in the wrong direction.

## 41. Attention for suicidal ideas and behavior.

A child gets ignored a lot by family members. The child does schoolwork fairly well and acts fairly reasonably toward people without attracting attention. The child mentions that she has thought about suicide. The parent gets scared, and very frequently attends to the child and asks about suicide and takes the child to a doctor for an evaluation. But after a while things go back to the way they were before, where the child is largely ignored. The child then does a "minor" suicidal gesture, which results in lots of interest and attention and solicitousness by parent and other family members and mental health professionals. Everyone all of a sudden takes the stance of, "You tell us what we need to do to have you be safe, and we'll do it."

Analysis: The child's baseline state is NAB, with probably some NUB mixed in – getting little attention for anything. When the child gets reinforced for suicidal thoughts and then actions, by her getting lots more attention and interpersonal power, that's RUB in its most dangerous form. Here an "ounce of prevention" in the form of lots of RAB, namely attention and recognition for her positive behaviors before all this started would have been worth much more than the "pound of cure" in the form of attention and concern contingent on suicidality of escalating seriousness. But even once it gets started, it's not too late for the parents to start RAB for admirable behaviors not related to suicide. It is conceivable that the causal link between this new policy and the suicidal behavior would reinforce the suicidal behavior, but if it more powerfully reinforces the admirable behaviors and establishes a good effort-payoff connection, the risk is worth taking, especially when contrasted to the alternative.

## 42. Nightmares result in bedfellows.

A child comes into parents' bedroom at 2 a.m.

reporting nightmares. The parents let the child sleep with them for the rest of the night. The nightmares occur more and more frequently, and the parents find that they have a bed companion closer and closer to nightly.

Analysis: Getting to sleep in the same bed with a parent or parents is for many children very powerfully reinforcing. This very powerful reinforcer follows the behavior of having nightmares. Could nightmares be a "behavior" that is "under reinforcement control?" Anything we do with our nervous systems, even when we're asleep, can be called a behavior; the working hypothesis should be that it is influenced by reinforcement unless proven otherwise. I've seen nightmares diminish greatly in frequency when the parents and child together decide to stop RUB and start NUB by letting the child go back to her own bed (perhaps after a little comforting from the parent that is not nearly as reinforcing as the parents' bed is).

## 43. Night fears are shaped toward higher levels by bedfellows.

A child comes into his parents' bedroom complaining of feeling a little scared. The parents are sleepy, and have the child come into the bed and sleep with them.

But they realize they may be setting a bad precedent. So they take the child back to his own room the next time he is a little scared.

But then the child shows up in their room really scared. They don't have the heart to send him back when he is so scared, so he sleeps with them.

Later they decide that they really shouldn't reinforce him for this fear. So they raise the bar on how scared he has to be before they let him stay with them.

Now, only when he comes in "out of his mind scared" can he stay with them. But these extreme levels of fear get more and more frequent.

Analysis: The word *shaping* is a term invented by B.F. Skinner, used by behaviorists to mean "reinforcing successive approximations to a goal behavior." You reinforce the small steps. For example, at first the piano student is reinforced for playing "Twinkle Twinkle Little Star," and gradually the bar is raised for the difficulty of pieces. Shaping is a great way to teach complex behaviors. But sometimes people inadvertently shape unwanted behavior, by reinforcing little steps toward it. In this example, the parents gradually required more and more scared behavior for the child to achieve the powerful reinforcer of being able to sleep with them.

In addition to getting differential reinforcement for high fear levels, the child in this case is getting intermittent reinforcement for the fears, which makes them more resistant to extinction.

## 44. Elevator exposures terminated when there's high fear.

A child has a bad fear of elevators. A therapist reasons that "exposure" to the scary situation is key to getting over fears, and encourages the parent and child to get on elevators together and stay on them as long as possible. The parent takes the child to an elevator for several sessions, terminating each session when the child starts crying and saying, "I can't take this any more." But the parent notices that the time the child is able to stay on the elevator gets shorter and shorter, and the child's dread of the sessions gets greater and greater. The parent concludes that this exposure idea is bunk.

Analysis: The therapist neglected to teach both of them that ending an exposure to a scary situation is a very powerful (negative) reinforcer, and that you shouldn't supply that reinforcer contingent upon concluding that you can't handle the situation. If the brain learns, "We'll escape the situation when the distress gets bad enough," the brain learns to *increase* the distress so as to be rewarded by the escape sooner. They are using RUB: reinforcing unwanted behavior. Is the child's emotion of fear able to be thought of as also a "behavior" that is under reinforcement control? Yes.

It is true that exposure is key to anxiety-reduction. But it's not just any old exposure: it's exposure terminated after goal attainment rather than exposure terminated when the going gets too rough.

## 45. Elevator exposure terminated after goal attainment.

A child has a fear of elevators. The parent and child go together to ride elevators, for a certain length of time, or until the child feels and acts significantly more calm than at the beginning (when *habituation* has occurred to some extent), whichever comes first, after a certain minimum time has passed. The fairly long exposures are repeated frequently, until the child's fear level is down to zero.

Analysis: Now the termination of the exposure session, which is still a reinforcer, is contingent on "goal attainment" rather than distress. Compared to the previous vignette, we have moved from RUB to RAB.

But what if the child is not yet at the level of "elevator courage skill" that the child can handle being on the elevator without running off? The next vignette deals with this.

## 46. Reinforcing courage behaviors in the same response class before real-life exposure.

A child is so afraid of being on elevators that it would be impossible for the child to stay on the elevator for a long-enough exposure, without the parent's having to physically restrain the child.

The child starts out by rating the SUD (subjective units of distress) level for various exposures other than actually being on an elevator. Simply listening to someone talk about elevators and their safety features is rated 3 on a scale of 10; looking at various pictures of them is in the range of 3 to 6; imagining being on the elevator with the door open is rated 6; imagining being on the elevator with the door closed and the elevator moving up and down is rated 8. Seeing a movie clip of someone entering and being on an elevator is 7.

The child starts at the lowest item on the

hierarchy and practices exposure to it for a long enough time that the SUD level falls dramatically. There is much celebration after this. The child gradually works the way up the hierarchy. Only after the child has gotten all the imaginary and virtual exposures down close to a zero SUD level do they venture onto a real elevator. Each fantasy rehearsal concludes with a celebration of the use of courage. Some of the fantasy rehearsals are "mastery" rehearsals, where one imagines that a miracle has made the elevator totally non-scary. Others are "coping" rehearsals, where the person imagines experiencing fear, but coping with it well.

From the beginning, the child is taught how to practice relaxation and how to control the speed of breathing. The child is taught to use helpful self-talk and mental imagery while doing fantasy rehearsals – to rehearse the thoughts that are least conducive to fear.

Analysis: Just as we don't begin swimming instruction by throwing someone into the deep end, we don't start courage skills instruction by throwing the person into the scariest situation. We start with easier tasks and work the way upward. The foundation level tasks are in the same "response class" as the eventual goal behavior, and so getting better at them prepares the child for the eventual goal. Each step along the hierarchy is celebrated; this constitutes shaping. A program like this greatly increases the chance for the exposures that decrease fear rather than those that increase it – that is, those terminated by "Hooray! I did it!" rather than by "I can't take it! Let me out of here!"

Going straight to the scariest situation and doing prolonged exposure does work, if the person is so motivated and disciplined as to be able to tolerate it. But in my experience one can avoid a lot of pain by using the gradual approach, particularly with lots of mastery fantasy rehearsals.

## 47. Learning to end hyperventilation-panic attacks.

Someone experiences panic attacks with symptoms of rapid breathing, heart pounding, tingling in the hands, trembling, nausea, lightheadedness, and very great fear. The person learns that hyperventilation, or breathing too fast, is very often central to these. The person learns that people who hyperventilate often misinterpret the unpleasant feeling they get from breathing a little too fast and thus having too little carbon dioxide on board. They often interpret this feeling as meaning they're not getting enough air, that they can't catch their breath. As a result, they breathe even faster. This creates a vicious cycle in which way too much carbon dioxide is blown off.

The person practices two exercises, called "hold the breath and correct" and "hyperventilate and correct." In the first, the person holds the breath long enough to feel just a little of the unpleasant feeling of too much carbon dioxide, and then corrects that feeling by taking a couple of fast deep breaths. In the second, the person purposely hyperventilates (say for 15 or 20 fast deep breaths), feels just a little of the lightheaded feeling that results from too little carbon dioxide, and corrects that by breathing very slowly for half a minute or so. Each time the person does these exercises, he or she pays attention to the difference between the two sorts of feelings: the high carbon dioxide state and the low carbon dioxide state. The person fantasy rehearses noticing a hyperventilation episode starting, but cutting it short by breathing very slowly. The person celebrates after doing each of these exercises, and the trainer celebrates when the person does them in his or her presence.

Analysis: Why not simply wait until the hyperventilation episode starts, and try to slow down the breathing then? One of the keys to successful learning is lots of reinforced practice of the desirable pattern. But in many cases it's impossible for people to practice the desired pattern in the heat of the moment. Sometimes the crucial ingredient for learning is practicing the desired pattern at some time other than when it's needed!

The celebrations of these practices constitute RAB.

I've seen a number of people completely eliminate panic attacks by such practice.

## 48. Reward offered for 7 good days in a row.

A parent offers the child a reward if the child can avoid a temper tantrum for 7 days in a row. The child starts out enthusiastically, and racks up 4 days in a row, better than the child has done in a long time. But on day 5, the child has a bad temper tantrum. The child, seeing that the 4 days' worth of efforts were in vain, resolves not to try for the reward any more.

Analysis: The loss of the expected reward can be thought of as PUB for the tantrum on day 5. But the problem is that now there is probably PAB, or at least NAB, for the 4 good days the child had. Demoralization is a very frequent result with "x days in a row" type programs. If the parent were to decide to give in and forget about the tantrum on day 5, this would reinforce the demoralized behavior and would teach the child that a deal made can be altered capriciously.

## 49. Reward for each good day and 7 good days total.

A parent offers the child a small reward at the end of each day without a tantrum, and offers the child a bigger reward when the child has accumulated a total of 7 days without tantrums.

Analysis: Now every day of tantrum-free behavior counts for something and is rewarded. The tantrum days are not rewarded. So we have RAB and NUB. This constitutes differential reinforcement working in the good direction.

## 50. Violent video games and martial arts.

A child has major problems with aggressive behavior. In his spare time, the child plays very violent video games. He attends karate classes frequently; the orientation of this particular class is on preparation for defending oneself against bad guys.

Analysis: "Shooter" games and many other violent video games provide opportunity for fantasy violent acts at very high frequency. And martial arts practice usually involves the rehearsal of fighting moves such as kicks and punches as a central activity. In either screen time or martial arts practice, children can get thousands of reinforced practices of role-played aggressive acts. Are these in the same response class as real-life aggression?

Let's say more about the meaning of *response class*. When we say that two behaviors are in the same response class, we mean that strengthening one of them, for example by reinforcing it, also strengthens the other. The two behaviors are similar in enough ways that there is *response generalization* from one of them to the other. For example, if a child gets powerfully reinforced for smiling at people and saying "Hi," he will probably also be more likely to smile at people and say "Hello." The two forms of greeting are in the same response class.

Now back to the child who plays violent video games and studies karate. Much research shows that fantasy and role-playing are very effective means of strengthening desirable behaviors. There are also many studies finding negative effects of entertainment violence. Despite some dissent and controversy, my reading of the literature is that those who claim harmful effects have a much better case. I also have seen so many people helped by fantasy rehearsal of desirable patterns that it is difficult for me to believe that people aren't affected by fantasy rehearsal of aggressive behaviors.

Scientific studies of martial arts are less conclusive. The effects tend to vary, probably because some teachers put a large emphasis on self-control and respect of authority and calmness, whereas others put more emphasis on proficiency in real-life fighting.

My conclusion from research and practice is that one of the most important interventions for aggression is to remove the opportunity for thousands of virtual RUBs.

## 51. Most fun first, or least fun first?

A tutor works with a child. Sounding and blending word lists is the least fun activity. Taking turns reading stories is more fun. And the child's following along while the tutor reads to the child is the most pleasant. The tutor contemplates what order to do these activities in the session.

Analysis: The tutor should probably do the

activities in just the order mentioned, from least pleasant to most pleasant. That way each activity will reinforce the previous one. Going in the other direction makes each activity mildly punish the previous one. We certainly prefer RAB to PAB.

Whenever someone prefers activity A to activity B, and does it more often given free choice, activity A can be a reinforcer for activity B. This idea is called the Premack Principle. By the same token, having to go from a more preferred activity to a less preferred one can be experienced as punishing.

## 52. Video games before or after homework.

Two children, in two families, have phone tutoring sessions and homework in the afternoon and evening. One parent lets the child unwind by playing video games after school, and also in the time between the tutoring session and the homework. The child is very resistant to stopping the video games for either the tutoring session or homework. The other parent lets the child play video games after the tutoring session and the homework are completed well. The child gets to play longer on days when there is a tutoring session than on days when there isn't. This child finds it much easier to start both activities, although the child tends to call the homework complete sometimes when it's not done very well.

Analysis: The first situation makes the homework and tutoring relatively punishing because of the contrast to the more reinforcing video games. The second situation uses the video games to reinforce the work. The first situation contains more PAB and the second, more RAB. However, because the reinforcer follows the decision that the homework is done, there's also some reinforcement of premature conclusion of work in the second situation. There may be a little RUB along with RAB in the second situation.

## 53. Video games before getting ready for school.

A child is having big problems with getting off to school in the morning. The child is in the habit of playing video games upon first arising. Then it's hard to get the child away from the screens, but often the child is hungry enough to want breakfast. Then it's time to get dressed; the child resists this greatly. The child is so resistant to getting his things together for school that the parent does this task for him. And walking out the door encounters great resistance too. He complies with most transitions only when the parent gets angry and raises the voice.

Analysis: The child does the activities in approximately the reverse order of preference. Each subsequent activity is less preferred than the previous, and thus each transition is probably experienced as a punishment. There is PAB for the admirable activities of getting ready in the morning. Each additional moment of staying on the previous activity that the child gets by resisting reinforces the resisting. So there is PAB and RUB. His compliance with the parent for getting angry and raising the voice reinforces this undesirable behavior from the parent, so the parent is getting RUB as well. The parent experiences the whole routine as very unpleasant, but out of desire to see the child succeed, keeps at it and does not give up. The parent admirably persists in doing the best the parent can do despite being punished for it regularly.

So parent and child are starting the day off with both PAB and RUB. A sad way to begin each day of life.

## 54. Video game after getting ready for school.

The parent in the previous vignette institutes a new deal for the morning. As soon as the child gets up, the child gets dressed, while the parent approves and sometimes even cheers for each step in the process. While the child is doing this, the parent organizes the child's things. When both these tasks are done, they celebrate by eating breakfast as soon as possible after finishing. But there is one junky but highly reinforcing item that is saved out (like a piece of sweet roll or doughnut.) In the time that remains, the child gets to play with a (nonviolent) video game for a while. When time to leave comes around, the child's reward for handling well the transition off the video game is the junky breakfast item.

Analysis: They are arranging the activities in approximate order from least preferred to most preferred, so that each can reinforce the previous one. The parent's social reinforcement for dressing, the delivery of breakfast, the permitting of the game-playing, and the delivery of the junky breakfast item all constitute RAB. The child's more pleasant behavior during this routine is RAB delivered to the parent. We all could use a little

RAB with which to start the day!

## 55. Parent finds the errors in homework.

A child does her math homework. The custom is that as soon as she finishes, she is to hand it to a parent who will check it, find her errors, and explain to her how to correct them. The parent looks at the homework sheet without a word, finds errors, and launches into explanation on errors in a tone of voice that the parent thinks is very appropriate but that the child experiences as disapproving.

Analysis: The child experiences this as PAB. Immediately after the child has done the admirable behavior of completing homework, the consequence is unpleasant. But the child continues to do the homework because the consequence of not doing it is even more unpleasant.

## 56. Parent responds to homework, version 2.

Another child shows completed homework to a parent. The parent first says, "Congrats for getting this done!" As the parent looks over the homework, the parent says, "You did this one exactly right!

What thought process did you follow to do that?" The child explains, and the parent says, "Wow, you've learned an important math principle!" The parent sees one that was done incorrectly, and says, "This one has an error; do you want to try to find it, or do you want for me to point it out?" The child chooses in this case to try to find it, and when the child succeeds, the parent says, "You got it!" On another incorrect one, the child says, "I don't really understand how to do this one." The parent says, "OK! I'll model how to do it, saying my thoughts out loud, and then you can do it, just the same way." The parent models, and at the end, says, "Hooray, I think I got it right!" The child then does the same problem, and the parent says, "You did it!"

Analysis: RAB, because the parent knows how to make the process pleasant.

## 57. Non-reinforcing the spouse.

Mrs. X puts in a day of work. When she comes home, Mr. X is already home from his day of work, and is watching television. He doesn't say anything to her, and she doesn't greet him. She starts getting some supper ready. When it's done, she calls him and he comes. He watches a television in the dining room during most of supper and goes back to watching television in another room as soon as he finishes.

Analysis: They both are using NAB: they are non-reinforcing the admirable behaviors of the other. Both non-reinforce the other's work to support the family. Mr. X non-reinforces, or perhaps punishes, Mrs. X's admirable behavior of preparing supper by his lack of any expression of gratitude or even interest. So there's more NAB and perhaps PAB. Mrs. X probably has a not very pleasant job of after-supper cleanup to do.

## 58. Reinforcing the spouse.

Mrs. Y comes home from work, and Mr. Y greets her warmly. He asks how her day at work went, and listens attentively as she tells about it, and says, "Thanks for doing that work for our family." She asks about his day, and they chat some more. She decides to cook something for supper, and he hangs around and chats with her and helps her while she does so. When they eat, he celebrates how good it is. At the end of supper, he suggests that they have a dish party, and they cooperate in cleaning up. When they're done, he says, "Thanks for having that dish party with me!" and she says, "Thank you, for doing it with me!"

Analysis: RAB from start to finish, in this vignette. Mr. and Mrs. Y seem to have a happy relationship. RAB going in both directions fairly frequently is an important ingredient for good relationships.

## 59. Punished by B's at school.

A student works hard in high school, and gets nearly straight A's, knowing that anything less will reduce her chances of getting into an elite college. In the elite college, there is a policy that only 35% of students can get A's. The student works extremely hard, and does very well, but 35% of the elite students almost always manage to do a little better. She graduates with a B average, and because of this she fails to get into the very selective graduate program she had set her sights upon; she feels that her career aspirations are blocked.

Analysis: She is in a PAB situation. Both her high school experience and the extreme competitiveness for graduate school positions lead her to consider a B grade as a punishment. Her rejection from graduate school affirms the idea of B as punishment. It is to her credit if she can avoid getting depressed, because a steady diet of punishment for effort is a recipe for depression. This is the opposite of the effort-payoff connection.

Of course, those who graduate from elite colleges with B averages are not doomed. There will be plenty of opportunities for work and school and major contributions to people. But it is sad that such an individual has such a feeling of failing and being punished, and that this feeling is not just a product of her faulty thinking, but of the system.

## 60. Bad grades in reading.

A child has a reading disability, and has gotten to third grade while remaining at the early kindergarten level of word recognition. He gets into tutoring, and works hard each day. In six months, he has improved to the first grade, sixth month level of reading recognition. But because he is so far behind his fellow third graders, he gets a low grade in reading. He takes the same standardized test that his fellow students take, finds it very unpleasant, and finds the results of it humiliating.

Analysis: The educational system is giving him PAB. The tutoring program probably is giving him lots of RAB, or else he would have gotten so demoralized that he would not have made progress at the wonderful rate that he did. We can only hope that the RAB from the tutoring program predominates over the PAB he gets in the form of bad grades and failure experiences.

## 61. Go away, brother.

A boy strongly dislikes his younger brother. He makes hostile and critical and inappropriate utterances to his brother, which leads his brother to walk away from him and hang out somewhere else in the house. The older brother says that this is exactly what he wanted the younger brother to do.

Analysis: The response of moving "away from the provoker," which the younger brother uses, is an admirable response, particularly in comparison to arguing back, hitting, screaming, and so forth. The younger brother gets negative reinforcement for this admirable behavior in the form of the cessation of the unpleasant criticism and hostility. For the older brother, if the younger brother's absenting himself really is a reinforcer, the older brother is being reinforced for undesirable behavior – RUB.

Sometimes, for children who are stimulus-seekers, the opportunity to get into arguments with a sibling is a reinforcer and the loss of this constitutes non-reinforcement or even punishment. If the younger brother continues the "away" strategy contingent on the hostility and the frequency of hostility goes down, we would infer that perhaps the older brother found the younger brother's presence reinforcing in ways he himself didn't realize.

## 62. Punishment for pooping in pants.

A child has "encopresis," which manifests itself to the parent in the form of the child's pooping in his pants. The parent punishes the child for this. The child tries to clamp down harder with the anal muscles that withhold poop, but this only makes things worse. The child starts hiding poopy underwear around the house.

Analysis: The parent doesn't realize that encopresis is usually caused by constipation and too much withholding of pooping. As a result, the reflex that leads to the urge to poop when the rectum expands gradually gets suppressed. A bunch of hard poop accumulates, and there is leakage around it or involuntary expulsion of it at random moments.

When treating encopresis, the main goal is not to get better at holding back poop, but to get better at recognizing the urge and getting to a toilet as soon as possible after each urge. More pooping, not more withholding, is the key to the cure. So the parent's punishment of pooping in the pants really is PAB. The child escapes something unpleasant by hiding the soiled underpants; we could say that the diminution in fear of punishment that the child experiences by hiding the pants is a negative reinforcer that reinforces this unwanted behavior.

So this unwanted situation is maintained by PAB and RUB.

## 63. Reinforcing pooping in the toilet.

A child has encopresis. The parent gives the child something (like Metamucil) to soften the stool and increase the bulk of it every day, and when the child complies with taking the bulking agent, the parent approves. There is a certain type of junk food that the child likes, and the child gets a dose of it, as well as celebration and approval, each time he poops in the toilet. (He shows the parent the result before flushing.) He gets a double dose of it at home for each time that he has the courage to go and poop at school; someone at school helps verify his achievement, and is approving also. The more he poops in the toilet, the less he poops in his pants, and he and his parent and the school personnel all find this outcome reinforcing.

Analysis: There is now RAB for taking the fiber supplement and for pooping in the toilet whenever possible, in the form of social

95

reinforcement, edible reinforcement, and eventually, the reinforcement that positive results bring on.

With anger control, the strategy of "get it out, don't hold it back," does not work, but with encopresis, it does!

## 64. Mom's praise seems punishing.

A mom and her son have been in large conflict. There is a high amount of hostility, criticism, commands, contradictions, threats, and insults, along with some physical violence that has been exchanged between them. A therapist advises the mom to start using praise for good behaviors instead. She does so. She then reports to the therapist that if she praises a behavior, the son immediately seems to stop the behavior, and seems purposely to do it less frequently from then on.

Analysis: It appears that this relationship has deteriorated to the point where the mom's approval is not a reinforcer, but a punisher. The son has gotten so thoroughly into the game of "frustrate the authority" that pleasing the authority is a downright undesired outcome. He would rather take revenge on her by displeasing her than to please her. Thus in carrying out the praise that the therapist hoped would be RAB, what the unfortunate mom is really giving is PAB. This is a very difficult situation.

In applied behavior analysis jargon, "establishing operations" are the things that can be done to make a reinforcer reinforcing. Withholding a certain type of toy makes it more reinforcing, and giving lots of such toys make them less reinforcing. Praise and approval from someone are not necessarily reinforcing without the "establishing operations" that create a desire to please the person giving the approval.

## 65. Mom makes her approval reinforcing.

A mom figures out that her praise and approval are more punishing than reinforcing to her son, because he likes displeasing her more than pleasing her. Similarly, she realizes that her disapproval has become a reinforcer for him.

After some study, she decides to cease her attempts to change his behavior by disapproval or punishment. If punishment is necessary, she is lucky enough that her husband can enforce it. She also withholds approval and praise for the time being, also, but withdraws somewhat from this child and pursues a positive relationship with his siblings. She tries to make all the contact that she does have with this child pleasant. When he does come to her with a reasonable request to do something pleasant, she often responds positively to this invitation, ending the interaction if he gets hostile. She doesn't do things for him or give him things, unless he asks her in a pleasant way, in which case, if it is reasonable, she does so. She and her husband plan that the father won't give the boy certain things, but will wait until he asks his mom in a pleasant way. Occasionally the mom suggests a fun thing for her and her son to do together, and if he refuses, she backs off instantly and waits a while before inviting again. She avoids unnecessary commands and works on the art of being a good listener and having fun conversations.

Analysis: The mom is trying "establishing operations" to attempt to establish her approval and her positive attention as reinforcers for her son. Probably the most important establishing operation is her cessation of hostilities that give her son motivation to take revenge on her.

## 66. Reading to a preschooler, version 1.

Person A reads a book to a preschool child. The person keeps her eyes focused on the book, and reads in a steady monotone voice. The child turns attention away from the book, and the person says, in an animated tone, "Hey, what are you supposed to be paying attention to now? Get back on task!" The more the person tries to read to the child, the more off task the child seems to get.

Analysis: We should use the working hypothesis that an animated tone of voice is reinforcing to the child. Have we ever seen a stage play or a movie where people speak in a monotone the whole way through? There is something built into our brains that doesn't find that entertaining.

If a monotone voice is non-reinforcing and an animated voice is reinforcing, the book-reader in this example is using NAB when the child shows the admirable behavior of attending to the reading, and is using RUB for the unwanted behavior of getting off task. This constitutes "differential reinforcement" in the wrong direction.

## 67. Reading to a preschooler, version 2.

Person B reads a book to a preschool child. The person makes as much eye contact with the child as possible. The person reads in a very animated tone, trying to act out the voices of the characters with as much drama as is reasonable. When the child turns the attention somewhere else,

Person B just sits back and relaxes. When the child comes back and wants Person B to continue, Person B picks up reading again right where she left off, again with great animation.

Analysis: If animation and excitement and drama are reinforcing, Person B uses RAB for the child's attending to the story, NUB when the child turns attention away, and RAB when the child resumes paying attention to the story. Person B is using differential reinforcement in the desired direction.

## 68. Parents celebrate the positive examples.

Some parents look at a list of 16 psychological skills, together with positive examples of each of those skills. (The list is: productivity, joyousness, kindness, honesty, fortitude, good decisions (both individual and joint), nonviolence, respectful talk, friendship-building, self-discipline, loyalty, conservation, self-care, compliance, positive fantasy rehearsal, and courage.) The parents prime themselves to watch carefully for any positive examples that the child does, particularly the examples of the skills that are of highest priority for the child. When they see a positive example, they 1) immediately respond with some excited attention, unless it would interrupt pleasant behavior or embarrass the child; 2) later, tell each other about the positive behaviors they have seen, often in the child's earshot; 3) narrate or act out with toy people the child's positive behaviors for that day, just before bed, in the "nightly review."

Analysis: All these are ways of using RAB without needing to count points, withhold foods or prizes, or do a lot of bookkeeping. These can make a huge difference in a child's life.

## 69. Fun after school refusal.

A child refuses to go to school, complaining of stomachaches and anxiety. When the child does not go to school, the child is cared for by a babysitter who comes over and watches TV and plays video games and lets the child do the same. The babysitter is an ice cream fan, and they have an ice cream party fairly often. The stomachaches and anxiety go away fairly quickly during these days. But they seem to come back more intensely and more often as time goes by.

Analysis: In the brain's unconscious calculations, it's certainly worth it to feel some anxiety and have a stomachache in exchange for getting a fun holiday from school. The calculations are not necessarily conscious – people can "decide" to become anxious or sick without even realizing that they are doing so. People can experience these bad feelings as coming out of the blue, unrelated to reinforcers. The child in the vignette is getting RUB. As we've mentioned before, we can count emotions and bodily reactions such as stomachaches and fears as "behaviors" that are influenced by reinforcers and punishment.

## 70. Back to school if better.

The parents of a school-refusing child decide that the child is having too much of a party on stay-home days. They make a rule that as soon as the child gets over the stomachaches and anxiety, rather than staying home with the babysitter, the child will head back to school.

Shortly after this new rule goes into effect, the stomachaches and anxiety begin to last until the end of the school day.

Analysis: One is tempted to conclude that the child is faking the symptoms to get out of school. But another explanation, in my experience more often correct, is simply that under this sort of arrangement the sick feelings are truly there, but are reinforced by being able to stay at home. Under the arrangement described in the previous vignette, only a short period of symptoms first thing in the morning sufficed; under the new arrangement, a whole school day of symptoms was necessary. The brain can learn to create symptoms to obtain important reinforcers, and those symptoms can be very real.

## 71. School refusal plan 3.

The parents and the child make a new arrangement, where the child will be educated at home for a while. The child will stay home each day whether or not there are symptoms. But there will be quite a lot of academic work to do. And until work is done, there are no edible treats, and no electronic entertainment of any sort. Reinforcers are delivered after carefully decided upon chunks of work throughout the day. Meanwhile the child works with a therapist to figure out the parts of school that are scary. Some of the fear can be reduced by practicing handling these situations in role-playing and fantasy rehearsal. These positive rehearsals are greatly celebrated by the therapist and the parents.

The anxiety and the stomachaches gradually

disappear over time. After some time, the child reenters school successfully.

Analysis: Now, since school is avoided with or without physical symptoms, we are avoiding the RUB arrangement where the symptoms must recur each day to escape school. The postponement of powerful reinforcers until the work is done constitutes RAB. As the child gets over the fears that made school so aversive, being able to stay home becomes not so strong a reinforcer.

Some children don't need a period of being out of school, and if it is possible to avoid any missed days from school, that's a different situation. But for some children this isn't possible.

## 72. The professor gets differential reinforcement.

A group of students in a class decided to do an experiment, using their professor as the subject. They counted and recorded the frequency with which the professor said the phrase "i.e." Then, the students, without being too obvious about it, started using contingent reinforcement. Each time the professor said "i.e.," the students looked interested in the lecture, nodded, and gave the professor eye contact. The frequency with which he said the phrase went way up. Then they went to the plan of not looking particularly attentive when he said it; the frequency went down. Then they resumed the policy of attentive listening each time he said it; the frequency increased dramatically again.

They finally showed him these results. He had been totally unaware either of their behavior changes or his.

Analysis: This true vignette illustrates that our brains seek reinforcement – in this case the reinforcement of the students' attention – without our always, or perhaps even usually, realizing consciously what we are doing. It's strange when experiments like this, from the behaviorist tradition, give evidence for the "unconscious."

## 73. Ignoring versus time out for hitting.

A boy at a day care center is hitting other kids. It appears that he looks for the teacher's attention each time he does so, and he gets it. The teachers decide to give him no attention whenever he hits, but to attend to his victim and make sure the victim is OK, or to attend to another child nearby who is behaving well. The rate of his hitting goes way down, but it does not disappear. In an attempt to make the hitting go away altogether, they decide to give him a "time out" each time he hits. But the hitting seems to rise greatly when they do this. They conclude that the attention he gets in the process of their giving a time out is more reinforcing than punishing. They use ignoring again, and the rate of hitting falls again.

Analysis: If their attention was reinforcing, the first condition was RUB, where attention followed the hitting behavior. Then the teachers went to NUB when they non-reinforced hitting. When they intended to institute PUB (hoping that time-out would be a mild punishment for hitting) they found that they had actually reverted to RUB (since the attention they needed to give in order to put the child in time-out proved reinforcing). So they reverted to NUB and held on to the gains they had made in that way. A good bit of RAB would have helped a lot – attending to this child when he is behaving prosocially.

## 74. The preschooler at the restaurant.

A three-year-old child is at a restaurant with several family members. The child is running around near the table. His mom says, several times, "Joshua, come here. Come back to the table, honey. Come back here, now." He looks at her, but doesn't begin to comply with her requests. After he runs off a little farther, his father goes and picks him up, saying, "OK, come on, my big boy." The boy gets a mean look on his face and hits his dad on the arm with his fist. His cousin says, "You get him, slugger!" and his family members all laugh.

Analysis: The continued attention he gets when he noncomplies with his mom's requests is probably reinforcing. And the attention and approval and laughter probably reinforce his hitting his dad. He's probably getting a good dose of RUB.

## 75. Picking a fight to rise in pecking order.

A boy purposely provokes a fist-fight with another boy whom he thinks he can dominate. He hurts the other boy in the fight.

In conversations with the boy, we learn that in the boy's peer group, there is a dominance hierarchy, a pecking order, of who gets picked on by whom. The boy consciously planned to raise his position of respect among his peers by hurting someone in a fight; he wanted to make other boys less likely to fight him. He felt that his strategy was successful.

Analysis: The improved position on the

dominance hierarchy is the reinforcer for the boy's otherwise inexplicable violence.

## 76. Reinforcement in the video game.

A child plays a video game. Every few seconds there is a choice that the child has to make. If the child makes the right choice, he makes progress in the game. If he makes the wrong choice, his progress is set back some. The child has learned to play the game well enough that at least 90% of the time he makes the right choices.

Analysis: We're not told whether the fantasy behaviors the child carries out in the game are admirable or unwanted. But the point of this vignette is that there is lots of contingent reinforcement – lots of effort-payoff connection. The feedback the child gets that signals, "You made the right choice," is a reinforcer. The rate of positive reinforcement that the game supplies is much higher than most other activities the child engages in. As a result, the child may spend lots of time playing the game that would be better spent in physical activity, learning, or social interaction. For many, many children the number of hours spent in video games is undesirable, and the very smart people who make the games highly reinforcing are hired to supply

RUB to these children. Others argue that kids are learning important cognitive skills by some video games, and the programmers are supplying RAB. The merits and drawbacks of any game are debatable. But the reinforcement that these games offer has vastly changed the experience of childhood from what it was before their invention.

A task of society is to provide for children somewhere close to as much of an effort-payoff connection for kindness and empathy as it has now discovered how to do with video games.

## 77. b's, d's, p's, and q's.

A student finds it very unpleasant to read. When a tutor tries to get the child to practice reading fairly easy stories, the tutor can not find a reinforcer powerful enough to overcome the child's aversion to reading.

A second tutor starts working with the child. The tutor finds out that the child cannot distinguish between b and d and between p and q with any more than chance accuracy. The tutor starts the child out by looking at pairs of arrows and asking whether they are pointing in the same or different directions. Each time the child gets a correct answer, the tutor clicks a tally counter; there is a celebration when the tally gets to a certain number. When the child has mastered this skill, the child looks at pairs of pictures and says whether they are the same, or whether they are different because they are mirror images. When the child has mastered this, he moves up to a slightly harder task, and progresses along a hierarchy. The tutor engineers that the child is successful on about 90% or more of the challenges, every step of the way. Finally the child works his way up to distinguishing successfully between b, d, p, and q 100% of the time. Then the child takes on the next step on the hierarchy for reading. The child is cooperative with this process and seems to enjoy it.

Analysis: No amount of reinforcement can lead someone to instantly perform a behavior that the person totally lacks the skill to do. But if you break the skill down into small parts, and figure out a series of small steps toward skill mastery, each of which prepares the person for the next one, amazing pieces of learning can take place over time. The set of steps, in order of difficulty, is referred to as the "hierarchy of difficulty." Reinforcing movement along those steps is called "shaping."

## 78. Big incentive to play the Polonaise doesn't work.

In a mythical kingdom, the ruler for some inexplicable reason wants to hear John Doe play Chopin's "Heroic Polonaise." (It so happens that John Doe has never studied piano or music-reading.) The king's behavior specialists expertly find out what John Doe's most tempting reinforcers and most dreaded punishments are. Then the specialists put the sheet music for the Chopin piece in front of John Doe at a piano and ask him to play it as written. No matter what reinforcers he is offered (including 10 million dollars, paid on the spot), or punishments he is threatened with, (including tortures too horrible to mention) he does not play the piece.

Analysis: This whimsical example is meant to bring out further the point made by the previous vignette. Rewards and punishments increase people's motivation or incentive to do something; they are not effective if the person lacks the skill development, and just *can't* do the behavior. A wise educator once told me that in her opinion, the most frequent error made in schools is mistaking *can't* for *won't*. In other words, the teacher thinks the child is refusing to do something that the child in fact doesn't know how to do.

It is possible, though not guaranteed, that if the person in our example started at the very beginning and studied piano for years, being reinforced for steps along the hierarchy, some day he could play this high-level piano piece. Perhaps in the next few days he could master a simple version of "Twinkle, Twinkle, Little Star." He needs to start with challenges that he can succeed at and gradually work his way along the hierarchy of difficulty. Sometimes when the strategy of "piling on more incentives" does not work, the strategy of "down the hierarchy to success, and then working upwards" yields success.

## 79. Overscheduled child.

A child is not doing well in schoolwork. The parents have tried offering prizes, attention, and praise not only for good grades, but also for well-done assignments. But the assignments don't get done well enough, and the child's grades are bad. They say, "Whatever reinforcement we give doesn't work for him." It turns out that the child is attending a school with demanding academic requirements. He is on a sports team that practices every day and leaves him very tired. He is taking piano lessons, and he is supposed to practice every day, but he shows up for lessons and recitals unprepared and gets a lot of criticism for that. He spends several hours a week in martial arts lessons. Because he is not doing well enough in his work, he receives tutoring. He complains that he doesn't have time to sleep enough or to do anything fun.

Analysis: Just as it does not work to pile on incentives for someone who can't do the task in question, piling on incentives also doesn't work for people who are so overloaded with things to do that their self-discipline reserves are chronically depleted. The fact that some people can thrive with a hard course load and many extracurricular activities does not imply that all people could be happy in a very high work and activity output if they just put their minds to it. Some people need more rest than others. Some have a lower intrinsic enjoyment of intense goal-directed striving. Some people need to clear their schedules of all but the most essential activities if they are going to be happy and successful.

When someone is expected to work at many different things, but is so overloaded that he doesn't get the reinforcement of a feeling of success at any of them, he is living under a condition of NAB, non-reinforcement for the admirable work that he puts out but that is spread too thinly. Bad grades and criticism constitute PAB. He's in a depressing situation.

## 80. Drug abuse 101 in college.

Parents send their child to college. He returns addicted to marijuana and alcohol. He wanted to have friends and be part of a social group at college; the group that accepted him put very strong and blatant pressure on him to use marijuana and alcohol to excess. For example, he incurred strongly disapproving and rejecting words if at a party he refused to take part in drinking games; he got lots of approval and acceptance when he did take part. As time went by, his grades suffered. He worried about failing, and the drugs temporarily relieved these worries. Over time, he used so much alcohol that he would get some withdrawal symptoms, which were relieved by more alcohol.

Analysis: The peer group supplies PAB and RUB, thus using differential reinforcement to lead him to use the drugs. The relief of the worry following the use of the drugs constitutes another (negative) reinforcer for the use of the drugs (more RUB). Finally, once physiological dependency has set in, there's another negative reinforcer, and more RUB, in the form of relief of withdrawal symptoms.

To send their son to receive this set of reinforcement contingencies, the parents had to pay about $60,000 per year.

## 81. Reinforcers for college work can't compete.

A college student has a problem with procrastination. He tries to do his academic work in his dorm room, but when he hears friends talking, he gets up and socializes with them, and finds that the socializing is more pleasant than the studying. He tries to write a paper, but instead he gets on the Internet and finds that surfing around is more pleasant than trying to write the paper.

Analysis: The pleasurable reinforcers of socialization and Internet surfing reinforce his turning attention away from his work. They are RUB. If the student goes to a place, such as a library nook, where the tempting reinforcers are not available, he will have a better chance. Removing tempting stimuli from your immediate environment is called using "stimulus control."

## 82. Reinforcing productivity at college.

A college student who has a problem with procrastination schedules for himself two hours of work (with a ten minute break in the middle) in a building on campus where there are no people he knows to socialize with, and no Internet access. Any other students who are there are studying quietly. If he is able to work productively for the two hours, he will let himself run back to his dorm and socialize with whoever is there, or surf the Internet if there is no one available to socialize with, for about half an hour. Then he will return to the building for another work stint, followed by another stint of pleasant activities.

Analysis: The pleasurable reinforcers of socialization and Internet surfing now are made contingent upon his being productive. He has turned them from RUB to RAB. Arranging for reinforcers that you control, to follow behavior you want to do more, is called self-management.

The difficulty in doing this, of course, is sticking to the deal of allowing oneself the reinforcers only when one has earned them. If one can develop the self-discipline to follow one's own rules about "I get this, only when I've done this," then one can harness the motivating power of life's temptations and minor vices to help one achieve self-discipline triumphs.

By depriving oneself of the reinforcers unless one earns them, one usually is doing an establishing operation to make them more reinforcing. This isn't a problem if the person is able to stick to the deal.

By removing himself to an environment where the stimuli tempting him to distractions are less plentiful, the student is using stimulus control. The student removes the reinforcers for unwanted behavior.

## 83. She works for a bad boss.

A woman works hard and does pretty good work, but her boss's style is to deliver nothing but criticism for errors and mistakes, and to threaten her with firing and give her disciplinary letters. She gets depressed.

Analysis: A classic case of PAB – although some of her work behavior is unwanted, the vast majority of it is admirable, but she gets nothing but punishment. A chief antidote to depression is a strong "effort-payoff connection," and a chief cause of depression is a setup where effort gets consistently punished.

# 84. Disability because of depression.

To continue the vignette above: the woman gets so depressed that she can't make herself go to work. She stays depressed so much that she gets classified as disabled, and gets payments for disability each month. When she starts getting disability payments, her husband, who had previously called her lazy for not working, accepts her disabled status.

Analysis: The escape from the hostile and punitive work environment powerfully reinforces her acting disabled and thinking of herself as disabled. The financial and interpersonal rewards also reinforce the status of being disabled. The combination of PAB, followed by RUB, constitutes powerful differential reinforcement.

Comment: Depression is sometimes conceptualized as a purely biological illness, treatable by medications, but for which some people are inexplicably unresponsive to medications. People undoubtedly differ in their biologic dispositions to depression. But if we don't look for the reinforcement contingencies, we may miss the most important parts of the story. Unfortunately, hostile workplaces, where the more powerful bully the less powerful, are extremely plentiful. In one poll, 35% of members of the U.S. workforce reported having been bullied on the job.

## 85. Food reinforcers in the tutoring session.

A child with major compliance problems goes to a tutor after school. The parent gives the child food and drink to take into the tutor's office. Periodically, throughout the session, the child distracts himself from what is going on by eating or drinking.

The tutor suggests that the parent put the food and drink into very small containers. The child will get a small unit of food or drink at the completion of each activity during the session.

Analysis: The tutor is attempting to convert RUB to RAB. If the child reverts to strongly practiced behavior of whining, demanding, getting angry, and refusing to cooperate when someone won't give him something he wants, the tutor will have to be quite skilled to avoid reinforcing such behavior. If the child goes through the whole session without earning the reinforcer and then refuses to go to subsequent sessions, the tutor will have succeeded in punishing the child's admirable behavior of coming to the session. When you want to convert RUB to RAB, you have to be careful not to stumble into PAB.

## 86. Aggression 101 in the day care center.

A non-aggressive child starts attending a day care center where there are several aggressive children. Another child takes away toys he is playing with, and when he tries to get them back, the other child pushes or hits him. At first the child submits to this. One day the other kid hits him, and he hits the other kid back even harder. The other kid goes away and ceases to bother him. The child experiences this a good number of times, and becomes more and more skillful in fighting. One day he sees a toy that another child is playing with, that he particularly wants, and he shoves and hits the other kid in the process of taking it away. He then gets to play with the desirable toy.

Analysis: Many people believe that aggression in self-defense is admirable behavior; the director of the day care center would probably classify it as unwanted behavior. At any rate, it is powerfully reinforced by the cessation of being victimized. But aggression in self-defense is in the same "response class" as aggression in offense. The self-defender practices aggression so much that he gets transformed into a bully. What is going on is RUB from start to finish.

## 87. Learning violence as a teenager.

A teenaged boy gets victimized several times by other kids stealing his food or his money, or purposely knocking him to the side when passing him, or verbally humiliating him in front of other kids. He studies mixed martial arts very carefully, and works out with weights, and gets a growth spurt as well. Now when people try to bully him, he stands up to them, often gets into physical fights, and is successful in hurting them without getting hurt badly himself. Each time he does this, he gains status among his peers.

He is interested in a certain girl. Another guy happens to be interested in the same girl. He threatens the other guy, and the other guy asserts his own rights; they fight, and he hurts the other guy.

Analysis: This is exactly the same vignette as the previous one, only the teenaged version: defensive aggression gets powerfully reinforced by its discouragement of bullies. But offensive aggression and bullying are in the same response class as defensive aggression, and thus they rise in strength in the behavioral repertoire. If we consider all violence as unwanted by society, the contingencies present RUB from start to finish.

## 88. Work block.

A student is trying to write a report. The student writes a sentence, and then thinks, "That's a stupid sentence." The student deletes it and writes something else, and thinks, "That's no good. If I turned this in, I'd get a D or an F." The student deletes what she's written and ponders starting out another way. But then she thinks, "I'm no good at this. It's no use." Then she decides to put off the writing, and she gets up and gets something to eat.

Analysis: A "big idea" is that we can deliver rewarding or punishing consequences to ourselves, in the form of our own thoughts, our own imagery, our own self-talk. The self-talk of the student punishes her admirable behavior of starting to write. Getting something to eat rewards her procrastination. We have the combination of PAB and RUB working to keep her from writing.

## 89. Overcoming work block.

The student goes to a cognitive therapist who teaches her about self-delivered rewards and punishments. Now she sits down to write. After the first sentence, she thinks to herself, "Hooray for me! I've gotten something down! I can always revise it later if I want to, but for now, my internal critic is turned off, and my internal cheerleader is turned on!" At the end of the first paragraph, she thinks, "That didn't take long! I've gotten some momentum up!" Then she decides rather than trying to write finished prose, to make a list of rough notes on what she wants to say. She thinks, "This is more efficient! Now I can focus on the ideas without getting bogged down in the wording! Good decision!" After some time of this, she has produced a very rough first draft of her essay. She rewards herself by getting up, getting a snack, and socializing some.

Analysis: She is now using RAB from start to finish. RAB is the key to overcoming work block. Again, the notion that we can reinforce ourselves with our own self-talk is an idea with far-reaching consequences. When she recounts this story to her cognitive therapist, the therapist is likely to be hugely happy and to deliver social reinforcement in the form of very sincere celebration!

## 90. Becoming anorexic.

A young lady is overweight, and gets teased and humiliated because of this. She strongly resolves to lose weight. She gets on a very restrictive diet. In order to increase her motivation, she looks at any fat on her body and thinks about how ugly and repulsive that fat looks. When she feels hungry and deprived of food, she thinks, "I'm doing something good. I'm doing what I should do." She feels good about herself. When she even thinks about eating a substantial meal, she envisions losing control, getting off her diet, and ballooning up again. She associates that image with strong fear of fatness. When she eats more than a tiny bit, she tells herself that she has made herself sick to her stomach by eating too much. She in fact does feel a lot of abdominal discomfort, and although it may not be worsened by her eating, she links eating with the discomfort. She loses weight and gets to a good level, but she keeps losing to the point of becoming horribly thin and endangering her health; she has anorexia nervosa.

Analysis: She develops her habits of rewarding self-talk for food restriction, and punishing self-delivered images for considering eating substantial meals, to do what feels to her like RAB and PUB. Associating feeling sick to her stomach with the act of eating feels to her like more PUB. And for a while, food restriction seems admirable and eating "normal" meals seems to be unwanted behavior. The fact that as she loses weight, she is no longer teased for being a fatso provides powerful (negative) reinforcement for the strategies she's using. However, she's unable to drop these strategies once she gets to ideal weight. Now the self-reward and self-punishment strategies become RUB and PAB, now that severe food restriction has revealed itself as unwanted behavior and good nutrition proves admirable.

## 91. A child punishes bossiness.

A parent is quite bossy toward her child. She issues commands very frequently, with a somewhat irritated voice. She directs the child to sit in a certain way, and corrects the child when the child doesn't do exactly what she wants. She tells the child to tell a third person about something, and if the child starts telling, she interrupts and says, "No, tell about the other part...." She directs the child to take the coat off when the child complains of still feeling cold, and to put the coat on when the child complains of still feeling hot.

The child becomes very disobedient to her commands. Sometimes he does not just ignore her, but does the exact opposite of what she asks. Later in life, the child looks back and says, "If I had done what she said, I would have been rewarding her for bossing me. I wanted to punish her for being so bossy, by not doing what she said. But I don't think it worked very well – she never got to be normal in the bossiness category."

Analysis: The child is attempting the strategies of NUB and PUB, by ignoring and defying the parent's unwanted controlling behavior. Like most human beings, the child had the capacity to keep on attempting the punishment strategy when there is unwanted behavior despite the absence of positive results from it.

One moral of this story is that if a parent wants compliance from a child, the parent should restrict commands to only the necessary ones. You want to avoid making the number of commands so aversive that the child can't stand to reward that unwanted behavior by complying.

## 92. Turning normal campers into an uncontrolled mob.

A camp counselor has some extra candy bars. He decides to hand them out at random to the children. But there are more children than candy bars. As he hands them out, the children push each other to get closer, grab the candy bars from the counselor's hand, scream "Me! Me!" to the counselor, and eventually start fighting one another. The counselor reflects, with some remorse, on how he rapidly turned a bunch of well-behaved children into a mob of misbehaving ones.

Analysis: The candy bars reinforce the grabby and greedy behavior. The counselor set up a RUB contingency, without predicting ahead of time what the results would be.

## 93. Learning internal reinforcement for reading comprehension.

A student participates in tutoring. The student and tutor alternate between reading and listening to short passages from a book, and the student answers a comprehension question after each one. When the student reads particularly fluently, the tutor often says something like, "Nice reading!" When the student gets the comprehension question right, the tutor almost always says something like "You got it!" or "Yay!" or "All right!"

Years later, the student is practicing reading comprehension tests. When she answers a comprehension question and is pretty sure she got it right, she notices that she says to herself, "Got it!" or "Yay!" or "All right!"

Analysis: External social reinforcement can become internalized. In other words, the student learns to deliver to herself, through her own self-talk, the reinforcement that the tutor previously delivered to her. The RAB that the tutor gave lives on in the form of RAB that the student has learned to give herself.

## 94. Vicarious reinforcement when the preschooler falls.

A preschool student sees another child fall down and start crying, after which the teacher picks up the child, holds him in her lap, and hugs him and consoles him. Not long after that, the preschool student falls down and starts crying, not far from where the teacher is standing.

Analysis: Did the student consciously think, "I think I'll fall down and cry so I can get the same hugs and holding that the other student did?" It's possible, but it's also possible that the student's brain made the calculation without the student's conscious awareness. And it's also possible that the event could be a coincidence.

But we are sure that there exists something called *vicarious reinforcement*. When we see someone else get reinforced for a certain behavior, and we strongly desire the reinforcement the other person got, we're more likely to try the same behavior as a way of getting it. Perhaps this is because the vicarious reinforcement incident gives us information, that increases our expectation that a certain behavior will result in a certain reward. The vicarious reinforcement in this vignette, by the way, is constituting RUB – since falling down and hurting oneself is unwanted behavior.

## 95. Attack ads.

A politician is running for office for the first time. The politician runs attack ads, even though the politician has never directly been reinforced for this behavior before. But the candidate and the campaign managers are aware of data that other candidates who have run attack ads have seen an increase in their support as measured by polls, shortly after the ads have run.

Analysis: Despite the fact that the candidate has never been reinforced for attack ads, he or she has been reinforced vicariously by the favorable results other candidates have experienced from similar ads. If we think that attacks and slurs on the other candidate's character are bad for society, the voters (or at least the respondents to the polls) are engaged in RUB.

## 96. Taxi Driver.

In a story reported in the news years ago: A young man (named John Hinkley) finds himself obsessed with desire for an actress (Jodie Foster). He repeatedly watches a movie called *Taxi Driver* in which the main character wins the affection and gratitude of a character played by Jodie Foster. But the main character wins her affection in a strange way: he sets forth on an irrational quest to assassinate a politician, but by chance he gets distracted into a different gun battle; he kills some people who had been meanly exploiting the character played by Jodie Foster; he wins her gratitude by saving her from them.

The real life young man gets a gun and tries to assassinate president Ronald Reagan, wounding him and his press secretary, James Brady. He winds up committed to a psychiatric hospital from then until the present.

Analysis: The vicarious reinforcement that this young man received through the movie probably strengthened the behavior of "attempt to assassinate a politician." We have no way of knowing what would have happened if he had never seen the movie; I would bet that his troubled life would not have taken exactly the same path.

Millions of other young men also saw the same movie without vicarious reinforcement's causing them to do something so abnormal. Did the vicarious reinforcement they experienced change some of their attitudes toward violence, just a little bit? We are dealing with effects that are hard to measure. But we do know that vicarious reinforcement often has a powerful effect. Because most people like violence in entertainment, the vicarious reinforcement we present to one another very often constitutes RUB.

## 97. Celebrity suicide.

A rock star commits suicide. There is a tremendous outpouring of respects and love and bereavement for the rock star, and admiration of what he did in his life. In the short time after that, the general rate of suicide in the population goes up.

Analysis: Vicarious reinforcement for the behavior of suicide seems to make this behavior more likely. Many individuals in society have gotten vicarious RUB. For a statistical report on this, see J Epidemiol Community Health. 2012 Nov;66(11):1037-42. Changes in suicide rates following media reports on celebrity suicide: a meta-analysis. Niederkrotenthaler T1, Fu KW, Yip PS, Fong DY, Stack S, Cheng Q, Pirkis J.

## 98. Compliance game.

A parent says to her child, "Let's play the compliance game."

The child says, "What's that?"

The parent says, "Are you interested in having this little bit of ice cream?"

The child says, "Yeah, sure!"

The parent says, "You can have it, for the price of 5 complies. Here's the first request: please touch your nose with your finger." (The child does it.)

The parent says, "Good! That's comply number 1! Could you please stand up and then sit back down?" (The child does it.) The parent says, "Yay! That was comply number 2!"

After 3 more quick complies, the parent says, "You did it! That's 5 complies! And here's that little bit of ice cream, delivered speedily!"

Analysis: The compliance game is a way for

the child to get "reinforced practice" in compliance behavior. The idea is to go down on the "hierarchy of difficulty" by giving requests that can be complied with very quickly and easily. Perhaps with enough reinforced practice complying, the child will have the compliance habit strengthened. People have used variants of this strategy in research studies, by giving a series of requests that are easy to comply with, to build up the compliance momentum before giving a harder request. To read about these sorts of strategies search on the Internet for the term "high probability requests" or "high probability request sequence."

## 99. Shaping game.

A parent says to a child, "Let's play the shaping game."

The child says, "How do you play that?"

The parent says, "I write down a behavior you can do in this room. Your goal in the game is to do it. And my goal is to give you clues that will help you discover it and do it. But the only way I can give you clues is to congratulate you or reinforce you for something you've already done. You just do things at random, and listen and think about what I reinforce you for."

The parent writes down the behavior, "Flick

the light switch on and off."

The child starts doing things at random. The parent says things like, "I like it that you stood up. I'm glad you're walking that direction. It's great that you're looking at the wall. I love that you're looking at the light switch! I'm so glad you're touching it! I love how you flicked it one direction... You did it!" Then the parent shows the child the words that had been written on the paper. During this shaping trial, when the child goes the *wrong* direction or turns to look at something that *is not* relevant to the goal behavior, the parent remains silent.

Analysis: Shaping is the reinforcement of steps toward a goal, and non reinforcement of steps that are leading one astray from the goal – a combination of RAB and NUB. When playing the game, the "shaper" gets practice in using shaping, and when the "shapee" does the goal behavior, that reinforces the shaper for using shaping well – RAB on another level. The shapee practices doing more of what the shaper reinforces him for; in general, being influenced positively by positive reinforcement is desirable, particularly between parent and child. So the shapee is experiencing RAB as well.

The parent and child can switch roles and the child can be the shaper and the parent can be the shapee.

If the players are lucky, their practice in the skill of shaping will generalize to using more positive reinforcement with other people, and to using more reinforcing self-talk to help oneself.

## 100. Feeling down does not produce a holiday.

A self-employed person gets up in the morning and for some unknown reason feels discouraged. He doesn't feel like doing any of the things on his to do list.

He considers taking time off and going out to eat and watching TV and surfing the Internet.

He decides that instead, he will make it a policy that when he feels like this, he will tackle the least pleasant thing on his to do list and get it over with. He congratulates himself for every step along the way in the unpleasant task, and feels really good to have finished it.

Analysis: For the behavior analyst, feelings and motivational states are "behaviors" that are subject to reinforcement control. If he were to reward himself for feeling down, by allowing himself a mini-holiday, he would be teaching his brain to feel down more often – this would be RUB.

By taking on the least pleasant task, he goes for PUB instead. But once he starts the unpleasant task, by congratulating himself for working, he uses RAB.

## 101. Child won't yield the video game reinforcer.

A child has earned 25 minutes of a video game as a reward for admirable behavior. But when, after 25 minutes, the parent asks for the game back, the child bargains for 5 more minutes. The parent agrees. When the parent asks for the game back after that 5 minutes, the child refuses to give it back. The parent lets the child play with it for another 45 minutes.

Analysis: The game initially was reinforcing admirable behavior – RAB. Then the child got reinforced, by more time with the game, for not sticking to the original deal, but haggling to hang onto it past the agreed upon time – RUB. Then the child is reinforced for the much more unwanted behavior of noncompliance by another 45 minutes with the game – more RUB. The net effect is that the child is getting more and more entrenched in the habit of noncompliance.

## 102. Incentives to yield the video game reinforcer.

A child earns time on a video game as a reward for admirable behavior. The parent and the child carefully plan ahead of time that at the end of the time, the child will have 5 seconds to hand over the game upon request. If the child does do this, the child will get one little piece of candy plus points toward a prize. If the child does not hand over the game within 5 seconds, there is no candy and no screen time of any sort for two days.

Analysis: The handing over of the game when the time is up is rightly seen as a very difficult act of fortitude and self-discipline which needs contingencies to instill it. The parent and child contract to reward handing it over with candy and points toward the prize, and to punish not handing it over by withdrawal of screen time. They are planning for RAB and PUB.

If they can train the child to comply with the very difficult request of handing over the game at the end of the time, they are then in position to use the game to reward admirable behavior. Until the child can comply, the game rewards unwanted behavior more than admirable behavior.

## 103. The math is over their heads.

A teacher goes to work teaching math at a school with very low average academic achievement. The teacher is given a standard curriculum that is meant to prepare the students for a standardized test. The teacher quickly learns that the standard curriculum is way over the heads of the children; they would learn lots more by working on material at least a couple of grade levels lower. But if she departs from the standard curriculum, she will be blamed when almost all students fail the standardized test, whereas if she sticks to the standard curriculum, she will not be blamed when they fail. So she sticks to the standard curriculum. Some students pay attention and try hard, but find it very unpleasant to work on problems they can't understand; they soon join the others in tuning out the math and trying to have fun defying authority.

Analysis: The teacher is negatively reinforced for the unwanted behavior of teaching at a level that is too high on the hierarchy of difficulty for her students – her reinforcement is escape from the punishment and blame she would have gotten had she taught at a more appropriate level. So she experiences RUB, and if she had taught at a more appropriate level she would have experienced PAB. The students who pay attention and try hard

138

nonetheless get a steady diet of frustration, or PAB. When the students take the test, that they will find it very frustrating even if they make good progress over the school year; they are experiencing more PAB.

Comment: Too often, once students fall behind, they get punished for being behind, and the punishment keeps them from catching up.

## 104. A school uses good hierarchyology for math.

A teacher goes to work teaching math at a school with very low average academic achievement. In this school each child is given an individualized math test. This test has items arranged in order of difficulty. The tester starts at a level where the child can get several questions in a row right, and keeps going until the child gets 5 out of 7 wrong. The tester says something like "Good for you!" when the child gets questions right on the test. The tester says something like, "You're paying attention well," when the child tries hard but misses a question.

The teacher is supplied with a list, for each child in the class, of what types of questions the child can and can't answer. The teacher is encouraged to teach at just the level of difficulty that will be not too hard, not too easy, but just right for the students, and is supplied with materials that will make this easier for her.

At the end of the year, the students are given an alternate form of the same test. When it turns out that most of the students made substantially more than a "grade level" of progress, despite still being behind the national averages for their grade level, the school administration celebrates and praises the teacher's work, and recognizes the students for their progress.

Analysis: Now the students find the testing a fairly pleasant experience – participating in it results in RAB rather than PAB. The teacher is rewarded for teaching at the right level of difficulty, and both she and the students get rewarded for the students' making progress and learning. There is RAB all the way around.

Comment: This scenario doesn't sound all that difficult to enact. But the scenario of the previous vignette stubbornly continues to be enacted, in my observation.

In this second "school math" vignette, the instructors were careful to choose the correct level of difficulty – the correct place on the "hierarchy of difficulty." The hierarchy is a series of challenges, arranged in order from easiest to hardest. The fine art of teaching at the correct point on the hierarchy, or "hierarchy-ology," appears to be one of the most neglected aspects of education.

## 105. Not allowed to quit piano without civil disobedience.

A student is at first interested in learning piano. But then she finds out that with the demands of schoolwork, she doesn't have time for piano, plus she doesn't enjoy it and is not very talented at it. She presents these ideas to her parents in a proposal that she quit piano. Her parents reprimand her for wanting to be a quitter and tell her to buckle down and work harder.

After a while the student refuses to practice the piano, even when directly commanded to do so by her parent. When the piano teacher comes, the student runs into a different room and refuses to come to the lesson. After a few times of this, the piano teacher strongly advises the parents to terminate the lessons, and they do so.

Analysis: The student engages in some rational decision-making and attempts reasonable joint decision-making, and gets disapproval for it — she experiences PAB. Then, her defiant behavior is negatively reinforced by escape from the practice and lessons that she finds unpleasant, and finally it is reinforced by her permanent escape from the lessons. By PAB and RUB, she learns that calm negotiation does not work and that defiance does work. Of course, we can debate: perhaps her nonviolent civil disobedience is admirable behavior, and it's good that it was reinforced. If it generalizes to further disobedience of parents, it will nonetheless be quite unwanted, in her parents' eyes at least.

## 106. Picture book models, contingent on unkind acts.

A schoolteacher has a bunch of picture books that the children like, which model acts of caring and kindness. When she sees an unkind deed, she takes a few minutes out of the lesson to read the children one of the picture books. She reports that the books always put the children into a good mood. However, the frequency of unkind acts in her classroom goes up as time goes by.

Analysis: It's great that the books model admirable behavior, and modeling is a very important influence upon us all. But the fact that the pleasant activity of story reading (and the break from probably less pleasant academic tasks) are contingent upon unkind acts' being carried out in the classroom makes this an example of RUB. The teacher would do better to make the story reading contingent on kind acts, so we would have RAB. If she were to save the most unpleasant activities of the day to do whenever there are unkind acts, she would be attempting PUB.

## 107. Voters reinforce sabotage of government.

There are two political factions in a faraway country. The prime minister is a member of one faction, and the other party has a majority in the parliament. The parliament members purposely enact policies that make the country worse off, predicting that the voters will blame the prime minister. They predict correctly; the voters vote the prime minister out of office and the parliament's party takes control.

Analysis: The voters rewarded the parliament's creation of bad conditions – they carried out RUB.

## 108. Mandated reporting reduces signing up for treatment.

A fictitious state makes a law that doctors and therapists have to report to the government any person who uses a substance that might interfere with the person's driving. The state also makes a law that that doctors and therapists must report to the state anyone who is dangerous to him/herself or others, so that the state can make sure the person doesn't have access to guns. After some time of this, fewer people with alcohol and drug problems, and fewer people who have violence or suicidal problems, go for professional help.

Analysis: Being reported to the authorities is an unpleasant consequence that punishes the act of showing up and asking for help. PAB is going on.

There are several states where regulations like these are in fact in place. I have not yet seen an empirical demonstration of certain people's avoiding treatment because of the regulations, but behavior analysis would certainly predict that this will eventually occur, once enough people are aware of the regulations.

## 109. A work party that really works.

Two students have a "work party." They each sit with each other and study, silently. After 50 minutes they take a 10 minute break, during which time they celebrate with each other their accomplishments, and chat some about other things. Then they do the same thing for another 50 minute stint followed by a 10 minute break, and then another 50 minutes followed by taking a walk together for half an hour. They enjoy the time they spend together.

Analysis: The whole arrangement is meant to reinforce the admirable behavior of studying. Each of the breaks reinforces the goal attainment for the previous stint. The socializing reinforces the work, and each of them reinforces the other for socializing. RAB is going on.

## 110. Work party with not enough work.

Two students get together to study. But after they have studied for a very short time, one of them interrupts the other to chat some. They start back studying, but very soon there is another interruption. They chat so much that they get very little accomplished, and they decide that they had each better study by themselves.

Analysis: If interrupting the work to chat is pleasant, then we have RUB going on – the socializing reinforces getting off tasks. The two people punished themselves by denying themselves future work parties, because they got off task too much – they experienced PUB. But they also punished the admirable activities of studying some and socializing a lot – there is PAB as well.

## 111. Unhelpful homework help.

A child asks a parent for help in math homework. The parent explains things so fast that the child can't follow the explanation. When the child then tries to do the problem, she does no better than at the beginning. The parent says, "I just told you not to do that! Why didn't you listen to me!" The child now is too upset to focus on the math, but the parent launches into another explanation. The child still can't do the problem, and now the parent is even more angry and the child becomes both tearful and angry back.

Analysis: Both of them are getting punished. The child is getting punished for the admirable behavior of seeking help. The parent is being punished both for the admirable behavior of trying to help, and the unwanted behavior of inexpert tutoring. We have lots of PAB, and some PUB.

Comment: If the child's instruction in math were optimized so as to be at the correct level on the hierarchy of difficulty, scenes like this would occur less frequently.

## 112. Telephone tutoring sabotaged.

A boy gets tutoring in psychological skills by telephone each day. An older cousin notices that this goes on, and without realizing it, feels very jealous of the positive individual attention the younger child gets. The older cousin teases and derides the younger boy's tutoring in any way he can think of – saying the boy is in love with the tutor, mocking the lessons by saying, "So today we're going to learn that being good is good, and being bad is bad," and so forth. The boy tells his parent he doesn't need the tutoring any more and refuses to go to the phone.

Analysis: The admirable participation of the boy in tutoring was strongly punished. The unwanted behavior of the older cousin was rewarded by his successfully sabotaging someone else's getting what he didn't have. So there is PAB and RUB going on. An alternative to this unhappy story would have been for the child to have a private place for the lesson with the older cousin not let in on it at all.

## 113. Sabotage of tutoring prevented.

A parent has enough wisdom and foresight to anticipate that an older cousin may be motivated to sabotage a child's telephone tutoring. The parent has a private talk with the older cousin before the cousin has even learned about the tutoring. The parent enlists the aid of the older cousin in reinforcing the child's work, just as the parents are reinforcing it. The older cousin agrees to help out. Then, when they hear encouraging or praising words from the older cousin, (such as, "Wow, I wish I could have done something like that,") they strongly reinforce the older cousin by much gratitude for his encouragement.

Analysis: Now the older cousin is using RAB with the younger child's participation in tutoring, and the parent is using RAB for the older cousin's helping out with the motivational system. Sometimes one brief conversation, combined with careful follow-up, can turn PAB and RUB into RAB.

## 114. Fashion snobbishness taught at school.

A child goes to a school, and tries to be kind and friendly to everyone. But the child encounters lots of derision from fellow students because the child is not wearing the fashionable kinds of clothes. The child becomes focused on wearing the right clothes. Later when other children come to school wearing the wrong sorts of clothes, the child makes snide comments about the other child's clothes. A peer who hears these comments joins in and agrees and acts as though they are in the popular group and the other child is in the unpopular group.

Analysis: The peer group punishes the admirable behavior of friendliness and rewards the unwanted behavior of fashion snobbishness. The behavior of adherence to fashion rules to avoid derision turns out to be in the same response class as deriding others for nonadherence. PAB and RUB tend to undermine the kindness and tolerance the child had upon starting at the school.

## 115. Bed as conditioned punishment.

A child has trouble sleeping. The parents' rule is that the child has to stay in bed, even if he can't sleep. He spends lots of time in bed tossing and turning and having very unpleasant feelings. Eventually those bad feelings become associated with being in bed so much that going to bed becomes a "generalized punisher." Now the child has even more troubles sleeping, and the child greatly resists going to bed.

Analysis: Having lots of bad experiences while lying awake in bed gradually makes negative emotion come as a *conditioned reflex* associated with being in the bed, just as the connection between food and a bell caused salivation to occur in Pavlov's dogs as a conditioned reflex to hearing the bell. This negative conditioning is an "establishing operation" that makes the bed punishing. The admirable behavior of going to bed at a reasonable time without a struggle faces PAB.

## 116. The payoffs favor sleeplessness.

A child has trouble sleeping. The parents and the child adopt a plan that when the child can't sleep for as much as 15 minutes, he will get up out of bed and do something else. The child chooses to play video games that he isn't allowed to play at other times, and to get himself junk food he isn't allowed at other times. He sleeps less and less during the bedtime hours and it is extremely difficult to get him to wake up. He also falls asleep in school the next day.

Analysis: Now there are powerful reinforcers for waking up and staying awake. Poor sleep is maintained by RUB.

## 117. Better bedtime plans.

A child has trouble sleeping. The parents and the child adopt a plan that when the child can't sleep for as much as 15 minutes, he will get up out of bed, but the activities he is allowed to do are limited. He may read books on school subjects, or books on psychological skills. He is also allowed to write about anything on his mind, or organize the things in his room. The light in his room is to be as dim as possible. The child actually cooperates with this, and begins to sleep much better.

Analysis: Now the activities that are an alternative to sleeping are some that pay off in the long run, but are for this child not pleasurable enough to reinforce sleeplessness. There is NUB, non-reinforcement of the unwanted behavior. Now the child has the chance for the bed to regain a conditioned association with the pleasant feeling of resting when one is really sleepy.

## 118. Ratio of approval to disapproval way too low.

A parent wants very much for her child to have good manners. At supper time, the parent nearly constantly corrects the child if the child has elbows on the table, chews with a mouth open, gets up without permission, fails to have a napkin in the lap, does not place the silverware in the proper position upon finishing, and so forth. Many disapproving corrections take place at other times, also. The child experiences this as quite unpleasant, and tries to punish the parent for it by being argumentative, speaking in very disrespectful ways, and defying the parent's commands. This leads the parent to punish the child by withdrawing privileges. The child responds by stealing back the forbidden privileges when the parent is not around to enforce, or openly defying the parent's commands to hand over the forbidden objects. The parent also notices that when she praises the child, the child tries to do the opposite of what he was praised for.

Analysis: When the ratio of disapproval to approval passes a certain threshold, the parent ceases to be a "generalized reinforcer" and becomes a "generalized punisher." At this point, the child is motivated to avoid the parent, get revenge, displease the parent, and disobey, out of a human instinct to punish the parent's unwanted behavior. There can easily get to be a vicious cycle in relationships where each person is trying to use PUB for the other's unwanted behavior.

To prevent this from happening, I recommend having no higher than a 1 to 4 ratio of disapproval to approval behaviors on the part of the parent – that is, of all the utterances that are either approving or disapproving, at least 80% of those are approving. This will go a long way toward promoting a "positive emotional climate," where people are using RAB with each other frequently and having a good time doing so.

## 119. Educational game can't compete.

A parent wants to take advantage of a really good educational program for a tablet computer. The parent buys the program, and shows the child how to use it. It is mildly reinforcing, more so than not playing with anything; it looks promising. As soon as the parent walks away, the child connects with the Internet and starts playing a violent video game.

Analysis: Highly intelligent game makers have spent their entire careers designing games that are meant to accomplish only one purpose: to make people want to play them more. Game makers who want to teach skills such as thinking before acting or academic skills are at a competitive disadvantage. When the devices that children have in hand can access any of these games with only a few touches, the unwanted behavior of abandoning the academic program and going to the excitement-maximizing one is strongly reinforced. We have RUB built into the device that we admired partly because of its multiple capabilities.

## 120. Educational game used more when competition eliminated.

In response to this, the parent goes on Ebay and buys a "retro" electronic device that will do only one thing, namely the academic task that the program for the new computer did. It is mildly reinforcing.

Analysis: Now the device furnishes some RAB if the child uses it, and NUB if the child turns attention away. At least it isn't an agent of RUB. The parent's attention and approval may be necessary as additional RAB to keep the device from gathering dust unused on a shelf.

The parent has found that "less is more" with respect to the multiple capabilities of electronic devices.

## 121. Vicious cycle of punishment among teen boys.

A child goes to martial arts lessons for years to learn how to defend himself from bullies. Now a teenager, when another kid at school verbally harasses him, he stands his ground, verbally attacking the other kid in retaliation. The other kid hits him, which gives him license to use his hand-to-hand combat skills. He soundly beats the other kid. However, the other kid, after recovering, tries to restore his lost honor; the other kid enlists a friend to gang up on the child and use an umbrella as a club to hurt him. The teenager resolves to punish this, and gets a chain, ambushes the other kid, and severely beats him with the chain. The other kid gets a gun and makes plans to ambush the teenager.

Analysis: The strategy of both of them is PUB. But punishment is unwanted behavior, which in turn motivates people to punish it. Thus there can be vicious cycles where each person, or each side, is punishing the other side for its unwanted behavior.

Often the intensity of the punishment escalates, as each hopes to punish the other badly enough to induce submission.

This vicious cycle is one of the major reasons for the invention of the rule of law. The government, or the society as a whole, punishes bad behaviors rather than leaving the punishment up to the victim to carry out through vigilante justice. For many, but not all, the strategy of punishing society as a whole for the punishment seems too futile to be worth trying.

## 122. Lucrative cleaning job, but only when there's a mess.

A mom offers her sons money to clean up and organize their rooms, and they do take her up on her offers. But she only thinks to do this when the rooms have gotten into a big mess in the first place. She notices that the presence of extremely great disorder in the rooms seems to be getting more and more frequent.

Analysis: Although she is providing RAB for the behavior of cleaning up, she is also providing RUB for the behavior of creating the mess in the first place. She could have avoided this by making her inspections and reward occur consistently, daily, and not contingent upon the creation of messes. But to do something routinely, every day, even when there is not an immediate problem, is very difficult for people to do, because they don't get much immediate reinforcement for it. If her sons were to express great appreciation for her inspections and rewards, perhaps they could reinforce her enough to maintain the consistent schedule.

## 123. Parental fighting has become reinforcing.

Two parents both use nearly 100% disapproving comments toward a child, as the child does toward them. When the child rides a bike or skateboard without a helmet, that behavior leads one parent to punish the child in a way that the other parent disagrees with. The parents argue bitterly with each other when this occurs. They notice that the behavior of refusing the helmet becomes more and more frequent, and they also realize that the other child behaviors that trigger arguments between them seem to be increasing in frequency.

Analysis: With enough data, the parents may be forced to acknowledge that their fighting with each other has probably become a reinforcer for the child. In that case, they are using RUB. Perhaps the parents' fighting is reinforcing because the child wants to get revenge on both of them. Or perhaps the child finds it reinforcing because while the parents are blaming each other, they are not blaming him. Basing incentives on RAB and minimizing the use of PUB could probably have prevented this outcome.

## 124. Child has a right to his own possessions?

Some parents have successfully used both money and working toward toys as reinforcers for admirable behavior in their child. The child's birthday comes along, and the child gets lots of money and toys as presents from some relatives who have recently become wealthy. The child is no longer motivated to work for money or toys. Someone advises the parents, "You can control the child's access to the toys, and you can control when and upon what the child spends money." The parents say, "Doesn't he have a right to them? After all, he does own them. If we try to control how he uses them now, he'll be furious."

Analysis: What the parents had use for RAB has become no longer reinforcing, because of satiation. They then doubted their own authority; they are probably correct that if they try to reclaim it, they are in for a battle. If they had established from the very beginning that although he may own the toys and the money, they are the ultimate arbiters of when and how he gets to use them, they could have continued to use them as RAB. But an even better solution would have been for the relatives to consult with the parents first, and to help out by supplying rewards to the child only when the parents certify that the child has earned them.

## 125. What stops the barking makes it more frequent.

A woman's dog barks loudly, disturbing family members and neighbors. The woman decides to try behavioral techniques. When the dog barks, she goes to the dog, puts her finger to her lips and makes a "Shhhh" sound. When the dog stops barking, she reinforces the dog with a little edible treat. She notices two things as time passes: first, that the dog stops barking faster and faster after she gives the signal; second, the dog starts barking more and more frequently.

Analysis: The treat, as well as the attention, reinforces the stopping of barking, but since the dog can't stop barking without the behavior of "starting barking" at the beginning of the behavior chain, the treat also reinforces starting barking. This is like several other vignettes where reinforcing "stopping behavior x" results in increased frequency of "starting behavior x." There is RUB going on for the unwanted behavior of "starting barking," despite the RAB for the behavior of "stopping barking upon command."

## 126. A different plan about the barking dog.

The woman from the previous vignette tries a different strategy. She sets a timer on her watch to go off every fifteen minutes. If the dog has not barked at all during the previous interval, she gives the dog a treat. After some time with this schedule, she lengthens the interval to half an hour, and then to an hour. The frequency with which the dog barks goes down.

Analysis: Now the woman is reinforcing any behavior other than barking during the interval in question. This is somewhat more difficult to carry out, but because we have RAB rather than RUB, it pays off if the trainer can stick with it. Behaviorists may speak of this as a DRO: Differential

Reinforcement of Other behavior than the unwanted sort.

## 127. Prolonged exposure to the trigger of barking.

Another person has a problem with a barking dog. This person notices that the dog is stimulated to bark by knocking sounds, for example anything similar to a knock on the door. The person makes an audio recording of knocking sounds and plays it continuously for an hour or more on several occasions. The person stays away from the dog during this time. At first the dog barks, but as the knocking sounds continue, the dog gradually stops barking, and goes and lies down. When the recording is played again, the dog barks for a much shorter time. Finally the recording can be played without the dog's reacting at all. The dog also stops barking so much at other sounds.

Analysis: It's hard to say what the reinforcer was for the dog to bark in the first place. Perhaps the knocking was a "discriminative stimulus," signaling the dog that barking would be reinforced by the human coming to see who was there and paying some attention to the dog. A discriminative stimulus is a signal that says, "Under these conditions, a certain response will get a certain reinforcement; under other conditions, it won't." Continuing the discriminative stimulus of the knocking sounds allows the dog to continue to do the behavior without getting reinforced for it. So the barking behavior undergoes "extinction" by being non-reinforced. The dog's behavior is improved by NUB, non-reinforcement of an unwanted behavior.

## 128. Well-meaning mentor overlooks vicious cycle of punishment.

In a novel called *One Plus One,* a well-meaning man teaches a youth computer hacking skills to get back at a bully who has been victimizing the kid. In response to being hacked, the bully physically attacks the kid's sister in retaliation for the retaliation.

Analysis: The well-meaning man was hoping that the strategy of PUB, punishing unwanted behavior, would work well for the kid who was bullied. Instead, it gave the bully an incentive to use PUB in response to the unwanted behavior of being hacked. This is another example of the vicious cycle of punishment for punishment for punishment.
As the plot continues, the bullying behavior is captured on camera, and the involvement of legal

authorities actually helps end the bullying. PUB coming via the rule of law is usually more effective than that coming by way of vigilante justice.

There are many, many examples that could be drawn from works of fiction – in fact, it's hard to imagine a story line in which the characters are not seeking reinforcement or trying to avoid punishment.

## 129. Disability payments for anxiety.

A person applies for, and gets, disability payments from the Social Security system because of anxiety severe enough to keep the person from working. As long as the person is too anxious to work, the disability payments keep coming; if the person should become courageous enough to start working, the payments would cease.

Analysis: The payments probably reinforce the unwanted behaviors of anxiety and work avoidance. (Emotions such as anxiety are treated by behavior analysts as a behaviors that are subject to reinforcement control.) If so, the payments constitute RUB.

Disability payment systems offer an ongoing dilemma – we want to be compassionate, yet we want not to give incentives for continued disability.

Some have argued that disabled people should receive their payments in a lump sum; that way the payments would not discourage recovery. But there are major problems with lump sum payments also. What about disability payments that are contingent upon the person's working hard to overcome the disability, and which would actually *increase* for a certain length of time if the person overcomes the disability? I've never heard of this system's being tried. But the answer to the disability dilemma may lie not so much in providing incentives to work, so much as somehow making job openings for positions that can harness people's skills and provide an effort-payoff connection. In a thoughtful report on the disability problem (http://apps.npr.org/unfit-for-work/), National Public Radio reporter Chana Joffe-Walt concluded that "Somewhere around 30 years ago, the economy started changing in some fundamental ways. There are now millions of Americans who do not have the skills or education to make it in this country."

## 130. Rewarding fathers' exodus from families.

A welfare system makes payments to the families of dependent children if there is no father in the household; however, if the father, who has a low-wage job, lives in the household, the family is not eligible for payments. A father lives outside the household so that his partner and his child can receive the welfare payments.

Analysis: Again it's hard to resolve a major dilemma: how to take care of those in most need, without giving harmful incentives. If a system provides strong financial incentives for fathers to exit families, the system provides RUB that may be very harmful.

## 131. Child teaches parent to scream.

A parent commands a child to do something. The child ignores the parent's directive. The parent repeats, louder; the child ignores again. The parent repeats louder still, and the child finally obeys. As this happens repeatedly, the parent has to get louder and louder, until the parent has to keep screaming at a level that hurts both the child's ears, the parent's ears, and the parent's vocal cords.

Analysis: The child's obedience is reinforcement for the parent. The child's obedience comes only after louder and louder yelling over time. Thus the child is *shaping* the behavior of very loud yelling by reinforcing successive approximations to it. The child is inadvertently carrying out RUB, reinforcing the parent's screaming. When the yelling gets so loud as to be painful, the child's obedience is negatively reinforced by the cessation of the yelling. That part is RAB, but the behavior chain that the child is being reinforced for starts with the child's noncompliance. The fact that the noncompliance does not cease implies that something is reinforcing it. Noncompliance is usually reinforced by the ability to continue a preferred activity rather than shift to a less preferred one.

## 132. Three noncomplies results in no screens.

A parent commands a child to do something. The child ignores the parent's directive. The parent enters a tally mark on her cell phone. When three tally marks accumulate, the child has "screen time" eliminated for 24 hours.

Analysis: This strategy attempts to use the sort of punishment that is called "response cost," or withdrawal of reinforcers, for the unwanted behavior of noncompliance. The strategy is PUB.

## 133. Reinforcement for report card grades proves ineffective.

A parent wants to reinforce hard work on academic tasks by the child. So the parent says, "I'll give you $25 for every A you get on your report card." The next reporting period comes 8 weeks from now. The offer appears to have no effect on the child's work behaviors.

Analysis: This strategy attempts RAB. There are some problems with it, though. First, the reinforcement is for most children too distant in time from the behavior it's meant to reinforce. The phrase "time gradient of reinforcement" refers to the fact that reinforcers tend to diminish in value the longer you have to wait for them.

The second problem is that maybe even if the child worked extremely hard, it could be that the child is far enough behind or the teacher is concerned enough with "grade inflation" that a grade of B or lower is as high as the child can achieve. The incentive is meant to reinforce work, but the grade is not necessarily an accurate measure of how much productive work was done.

## 134. Nightly reinforcement for academic work, works.

A parent wants to reinforce hard work on academic tasks. The parent arranges to check out, each night, how well the child did on homework and how well the child is prepared for tests. The child gets a rating from 0 to 5 from the parent each night on the quantity and quality of the child's work (0=none, 1=a little, 2=some, 3=pretty much, 4=very much, 5=extremely much.) The parent has a roll of dimes, and drops anywhere from 0 to 5 dimes into the child's bank each night depending upon how hard and how cooperatively the child worked. The parent also tries as hard as possible to make the interaction fun, and to be nice and noncritical with the child, even when the rating is lower, and to generate lots of excitement when there are high ratings. The parent is careful to reinforce the child's sincere effort and not just the quality of the product.

Analysis: The reinforcer now follows the desired behavior in time, almost immediately. The pleasant social behaviors reinforce the child for cooperating with the checking, even if the work itself is not very reinforcement-worthy. The RAB in this case is likely to have a positive effect.

## 135. Anti-grade inflation leads to anti-cooperation.

The administration of a certain elite university gets worried about grade inflation and issues a guideline to faculty that no more than 35% of students in any course should get A's.

Astute observers notice that over time, students are less willing to cooperate with each other in study groups. Students are less often helpful in explaining things to other students who don't understand. Students refuse to share their notes with other students who had to miss a class because of illness. Students also tend to like their classmates less.

Analysis: The students have been pitted in competition with one another. The competitive situation makes other students' poorer performances reinforcing, because they mean a higher ranking for oneself. Helping other students can be punished by lowering one's own ranking. There is PAB and RUB going on.

## 136. A good job years from now isn't reinforcing now.

A certain reinforcement contingency applies

to a cohort of youths: if they work hard during high school and college so as to improve their academic performance, they will be more likely to get a good job after graduation. Yet a very large portion of them do not work very hard, but spend their time playing video games, partying, using drugs or alcohol, and so forth.

Analysis: This is a "time gradient of reinforcement" issue. The tempting activities provide their reinforcement right away; the reinforcement of a better job after graduation is delayed over a course of years. Those who tend to succeed the most tend to have internalized rewards that are more immediate, such as the self-talk of, "Hooray, I did some good work on this assignment!" or "I really knew what I was doing on that test!" RAB that is very delayed can't by itself compete very well with RUB that is more immediate.

Some people are more influenced by the expectation of reinforcers in the distant future than other people. Those who are more reactive to distant consequences tend to have more self-discipline. But most of them have probably found ways to make the reinforcers more immediate, by imagery or self-talk.

## 137. Tried a sticker chart and it didn't work.

Some parents start a behavioral program for their child. They make a chart for each day, and when the child has had a good day, they put a sticker in the space for that day. At first the child seems excited and pleased to get the stickers. But after a while the pleasure and excitement seem to wear off, and the child doesn't even pay attention when the parents award the sticker or withhold it for the day.

Analysis: At first, the stickers seem to have some reinforcing value, probably because of their novelty. But after a while, the novelty tends to wear off. The process by which a stimulus that brings out a certain emotional response gradually ceases to bring out as much emotion, the more times and the longer it is presented, is called *habituation*. Habituation means about the same thing as "getting used to it." Habituation is extremely useful when one is getting over unwanted fears and aversions. It is disappointing to parents when they think they have a reinforcer that will motivate the child, and find that the motivating power quickly decreases.

If the stickers were used as markers in a count toward a reinforcer that the child was highly motivated for, such as a toy, an outing, ability to play a highly desirable game, access to a highly reinforcing but otherwise inaccessible food, or so forth, then the stickers would gradually take on *secondary reinforcing* properties. A *secondary reinforcer* is something that becomes rewarding by being associated with something else that is already reinforcing, which is called a *primary reinforcer.*

## 138. Token economy for a child.

Parents set up a program wherein a child gets a point for each "comply" with a request or command from the parent, and also for any kind or helpful acts that were not requested. The child also gets a point for every half-hour that the child's behaviors do not include hostility or defiance. The child can buy a piece of junk food for a small number of points, and a toy for more points, and a more expensive item for more points. What the child can earn with the points changes over time depending upon what is most motivating for the child.

Analysis: The points are secondary reinforcers, and they are linked to primary reinforcers in the form of edibles and playthings. This sort of system is called the *token economy.* It is meant to provide RAB. The major problem with the token economy is that it takes too much work for most parents to be able to sustain it.

## 139. Checking the behavior records when deciding on a discretionary reinforcer.

Some parents make a chart where at the end of every day, they enter a number rating the overall level of the child's functioning during the time they were with her that day – 0 is very poor functioning and 10 is very good functioning. If she is curious, they tell her the number; if she isn't, they just enter it. They keep a backup of the numbers in case the child in a moment of anger should want to destroy the chart.

The parents also establish the custom that important reinforcers are not freely available, but the child must ask for them and get them only if the parents actively furnish them.

Whenever the child asks for something discretionary, that is something that is not a necessity – trips anywhere, food items, toys, time to play with toys, screen time, the parents look at the chart. They tend to say "Yes" if the recent ratings are high, and "Not now" if the recent ratings are low. Sometimes they say something like, "Yes, I'll be glad to offer that as part of the celebration when you have accumulated 5 (or a different number) more ratings of 7 or above."

Analysis: "Contingent reinforcement for good behavior" exists when there is a high correlation between how well the child behaves and how much the child gets of what he or she wants. This program attempts to furnish this. It incorporates several aspects that are necessary for such a program to work: the secondary reinforcers (daily ratings) are linked to primary reinforcers that the child strongly desires. The parents have gotten control over those reinforcers, to prevent satiation. The parents plan ahead so that any rebellion against the program doesn't stop it from operating. Another benefit of such a program is that it is simple enough to sustain, whereas more complex programs such as token economies require so much labor that parents are very seldom able to keep such programs going very long.

## 140. Social behavior of testers.

Two testers give an individual intellectual ability test to young children. The tester tries to maintain a "poker face" and monotone voice so as not to give any clue to the children and not to deviate from totally standard procedure. A different tester, giving the same test, responds with great enthusiasm to the child's responses.

Analysis: The first tester is using conditions of NAB, non-reinforcing the children's admirable behavior in complying with the test. The second is using RAB. It could be that the first tester is not measuring the children's intellectual or academic abilities, so much as how fast the child undergoes *extinction*. Extinction, as we've said before, is a gradual dropoff in the frequency or strength of a response as that response gets repeated without reinforcement.

## 141. What's the bully's reward?

One person bullies another to get food and money from the other person. But another person bullies another person with no apparent reinforcement other than the complaints and objections and protests of the person who is bullied.

Analysis: Why does so much bullying go on without any obvious reward for cruel behavior? It could be that signs that we are dominant over another human being are primary reinforcers for most human beings. In other words, people like being the top dog, being one up, winning, dominating, and they tend to admire other people who do so, even when such dominance accomplishes nothing. How else can we explain why people spend so much time in competitive games, and put so much importance upon being connected with a winning team? Why else would people admire boxers and mixed martial arts champions, who engage in fights for no sensible reason other than to have a dominance contest?

## 142. Shooter versus chess.

One person spends huge numbers of hours playing a "shooter" video game; another spends equally many hours playing chess. The first person makes gains in measures of reaction time, i.e. how fast the person can react to a certain stimulus. The second person gains in thinking before acting, considering several options, predicting consequences, planning ahead – decision-making skills.

Analysis: The number of reinforced trials we have had of a certain behavior greatly influences the frequency or the strength of that behavior in our repertoire. Some games tend to reinforce quick reactions, whereas others reinforce careful decisions. Life, in my observation, usually tends to reinforce careful decisions more than quick reactions, and this is one reason that chess is better for children than shooter games. (Another is that shooter games also reinforce the fantasy of cruel behavior. Chess is also a dominance struggle analogous to warfare, but the contest is much more abstract.) The extent to which skills of careful decision-making which are improved by chess practice generalize to good decision-making in life choices has been the subject of some research but could use more.

## 143. Legalizing a reinforcing drug.

A country legalizes the sale and use of a previously illegal recreational drug (e.g. alcohol, marijuana). The frequency of illegal sales of the drug falls, and the number of people addicted to the drug increases.

Analysis: The punishment for buying and using the drug is eliminated, and thus the behavior of buying and using becomes more frequent because it is less punished. The drug dealers or bootleggers find that their clientele already have enough of the drug; what they are offering is no longer very reinforcing, because the clientele is already satiated, i.e. has enough of it, obtainable by legal channels. Thus the unwanted behavior of selling illegally is less reinforced – NUB for that, but the unwanted behavior of buying legally is not punished – the PUB goes away, and the reinforcing qualities of the drug itself, for addicted people, constitute powerful RUB.

## 144. At school with a video game.

A parent sends a child to school with a hand-held video game to play when he gets bored. The child gets off task while trying to do schoolwork.

Analysis: The video game is programmed to give responses that reinforce attention to it (and thus directing attention away from competing activities such as schoolwork). The video game provides RUB – reinforcement for the unwanted behavior of getting off task at school.

## 145. Teacher demands compliance, then gives in.

A child plays a hand-held video game at school. The teacher, seeing that the child is distracting himself with it, directs the child to hand it over until the end of the school day. The child refuses. The teacher repeats the request several times, and the child refuses and keeps on playing the game. The teacher decides to ignore the off-task behavior and work with the other children who are on task. The other children observe this incident with interest.

Analysis: Getting to play with the game is a reinforcer, and quite a powerful one. At first, what is reinforced is getting off task and not paying attention to schoolwork. But once the teacher makes the demand to hand it over, the child's continuing to get to play with the game reinforces the child's direct defiance of the teacher's directive. The other children in the classroom, who see that the child gets reinforced for defiance, receive *vicarious reinforcement* for defiance. Without a plan to enforce a directive, giving the directive often does more harm than good.

## 146. Getting reinforcers by breaking rules.

A kid wants fashionable clothes so much that he steals the money to get them rather than working for the money. And: A child is on a contingency program where he earns screen time by attaining a high daily rating, but he wants to play video games so much that he gets up in the middle of the night when his parents are asleep and plays them. And: Someone wants a good grade on a test so much that he devises a clever way of bringing notes into a test and looking at them without being detected. And: A person wants to make money in the stock market so much that he manages to get inside information that isn't available to the public, and uses it to make a profit when the stock market reacts to big news.

Analysis: Fashionable clothes, screen time, good grades, and money are in these examples very powerful reinforcers. If the people in question "played by the rules," and behaved honestly, these reinforcers could have motivated them toward productive work or good behavior – they could have been RAB. But instead, the reinforcers all constitute RUB for dishonest behavior. Many people don't think about one of the main advantages of honesty: it allows an effort-payoff connection that is destroyed when one gets the payoff without the right type of effort. And one of the main challenges in teaching honesty skills is that stealing reinforcers usually takes less effort than working for them.

## 147. Employers as criminals.

A person starts a small business and employs several people in an activity that he thinks will meet a need and make the world a better place. He immediately gets fined because he didn't buy worker's compensation insurance on time. He gets in trouble with the law for not collecting the correct documents to make sure that the workers were not illegal immigrants. He asks a prospective employee if the employee has a criminal history, and by doing so, he becomes a criminal himself, because his state has made such a question illegal to ask at a certain stage of the hiring process. Several other people hear about what happened to him and resolve not to start a business that requires having employees.

Analysis: If we assume that the business owner is right about the positive benefits to society from the work his company hopes to carry out, then the admirable behavior of trying to carry out this task is punished by the mandates on employers. Other prospective employers avoid becoming employers because of vicarious punishment. Lots of PAB is going on. It would not be too far-fetched to imagine that these punishment contingencies have an effect upon the availability of jobs in the society.

## 148. The viewing public reinforces rudeness.

A current events show on television has low ratings. The producer encourages and goads the guests to get really mad at each other and to have big arguments. The ratings improve. More and more shows of this sort become shouting matches.

Analysis: The ratings are a very powerful reinforcer for the producers. The viewers appear to prefer to watch loud arguments than conversations involving calm reasoning, and they change the behavior of the participants in the show by the reinforcement they provide by watching. The viewers are engaging in RUB, even though some of them also complain about the low level of civility in the programs they are watching. This RUB has a vicarious effect upon producers of other shows who study what sorts of behaviors get higher ratings.

## 149. A tutor keeps on until the student refuses.

A child has tutoring sessions. The tutor wants to push on with self-discipline requiring activities, because they promote great progress in the child's learning. The child starts to whine that he is tired of doing this particular activity, and says, "Can we stop?" The tutor pushes on a little further, until the child says, "I'm not doing this any more! I hate this." The tutor then says "OK, let's do something else." They then go to an activity that the child likes better.

Analysis: The stopping of the first activity is clearly a reinforcer for the child (a negative reinforcer, because it's the stopping of something unpleasant). It reinforces the behavior that it follows, namely the child's refusal to continue and expression of strong negative feelings about the activity. We might predict that the refusal and the expression of negative feelings will occur sooner and more frequently in future sessions, because of the RUB the child receives.

## 150. A tutor keeps on until there's goal attainment.

A child has tutoring sessions. The tutor knows that a certain activity requires self-discipline from the child, but it very much promotes progress in important skills. The tutor sets a goal with the child where they will get a certain number of "points" worth of progress, after which they will very joyously celebrate the child's self-discipline and go on to the next activity, which is more pleasant. The tutor is very careful to set the goal at a level that the child currently has the work capacity to handle. Over time, the work load very gradually increases.

Analysis: In this circumstance, the ending of the self-discipline requiring activity, which is still a reinforcer, reinforces *task completion* or *goal attainment* rather than *task rejection*. The difference between this scenario and the one in the previous vignette may not be striking to the casual observer, but the difference in outcomes can be enormous. The difference is that the ending of the activity is now RAB instead of RUB.

## 151. Treating irritability with food.

A child experiences episodes of being very irritable – refusing to comply, refusing to listen to what anyone says, knocking things over, sometimes hitting. The parent has read that irritability can be a consequence of low blood sugar. So whenever the child has one of these episodes, the parent hurries to get the child some food. The child tends to be picky about what he will accept during these episodes, so the parent offers whatever the child will accept: a cookie, a candy bar, or some apple juice. The child's behavior usually improves pretty dramatically when the child is fed. However, the frequency of the episodes steadily increases over time.

Analysis: There's little doubt that the food the child receives is reinforcing, and that the behavior that it follows is undesirable. RUB is certainly going on. If the child really is having episodes of low blood sugar, then the best strategy would be to offer nutritious snacks at regular intervals, avoiding as much as possible the simple sugars that provoke a major insulin response that then leads to a rebound low blood sugar. However, it would be very desirable to test and see whether the child's blood sugars are abnormal in the first place. One strategy involves doing blood tests immediately when the episodes begin. Another strategy is testing during a prolonged fast. Consultation with a pediatric endocrinologist may be a good idea.

## 152. Irritability results in a blood test.

A child has suspected episodes of low blood sugar, with symptoms primarily of irritability. The child is asked to report when he has other symptoms, such as shakiness, heart pounding, strong hunger, dizziness, and so forth. When the child gets either irritable or reports any of the other symptoms, he gets a blood test. The blood tests are painful.

Analysis: The blood tests now punish the unwanted behavior of the destructive, aggressive, and defiant behavior. They also punish the admirable behavior of verbally reporting symptoms. So both PUB and PAB are going on.

## 153. "Stop that!" without follow-up.

A parent talks with another adult, while her children play. When they do things that are perhaps dangerous or very loud or hostile to one another or possibly destructive of property, the parent yells at the kids to stop. Then she turns her attention back to the conversation with the other adult. The frequency of the unwanted behaviors seems to increase over time.

Analysis: For many children, getting noticed by the parent is a reinforcer, not a punishment. The excited commands to stop doing something are RUB. For many of them, verbalizations that are louder, higher in pitch, and faster are even more reinforcing, because they convey excitement. When excitement is more reinforcing, we say that the child is more "stimulus-seeking."

## 154. We interrupt this conversation for RAB.

A parent talks with another adult, while children are playing. She has trained herself to notice when they laugh and have fun together while doing something harmless. When they do, she sometimes yells at them, in an excited voice, "Hey!

I want to hear about what's funny! I need more funniness in my life!" She does this after making a quick decision about whether interrupting them in this way would be pleasant or unpleasant for them. She notices that over time they have more fun with each other.

Analysis: Now she is using her excitement to reinforce behavior she finds admirable; instead of RUB there is RAB.

## 155. The researcher discovers: excitement is reinforcing.

Someone does a research paper, and tries to tally up the total amount of money spent on entertainment meant to increase the excitement level of the people purchasing the entertainment. By the time the person adds up the revenues and expenditures on of scary/exciting amusement park rides, scary and violent movies, books, and plays, songs that deal with taboo or otherwise exciting topics, car racing, violent sports competitions, very loud rock concerts, and violent or otherwise exciting video games, the person figures that enough money is spent to fund psychoeducation for every child on the planet.

Analysis: This vignette is meant to provide some evidence for us that excitement is, as a general rule, reinforcing. The excitement need not be about something "positive" to be reinforcing. Why else would we spend huge sums of money and huge amounts of time on depictions of horrible things happening to other human beings? The message is that parents should usually try to inhibit the natural response of getting excited about children's misbehavior, out of a desire not to provide RUB.

## 156. Stimulus-seeking incident at the cinema.

Four adolescents are sitting together in a movie theater. They make loud and boisterous comments and noises in reaction to to the events in the movie. Some other audience members sitting nearby try to shush them. They make hostile commands to "Shut up" when the adolescents make noise. This triggers hostile and defiant comments in response, as well as laughter, and increased frequency of noise. When the movie ends, the two groups yell at each other and then get into a physical fight.

Analysis: The excitement the noise generates appears to reinforce rather than punish the noise-making behavior. The four adolescents are getting RUB. But why did the second group not simply ask the manager to control the noise level, or move to the other end of the theater? It could be that the exchange of hostile words and the excitement generated was reinforcing to the second group of people as well. If excitement is a reinforcer for both of them, they mutually reinforce each other for hostility and anger.

If it were not for the PUB usually delivered to at least one person by the physical fight, the RUB that occurs when excitement generates hostility might generate many more hostile interchanges. The ability to be hostile with no chance of getting a black eye (or a lawsuit for giving someone else a concussion) may be one reason why people's anonymous interactions on the Internet so often degenerate into hostile insults.

## 157. When should the babysitter offer the snack?

A parent gives instructions to a babysitter. The parent says, "When these guys get too unruly and out of control, giving them a snack will usually make them calm down." The babysitter, an expert at applied behavior analysis, smiles sweetly and nods, but later says to the boys, "We'll have a snack maybe to celebrate how nice you've been to each other and to me!" The parent is regularly amazed to hear how cooperative the boys are with the babysitter.

Analysis: The parent is advising the use of RUB, whereas the babysitter is choosing to use RAB instead. It is not just this single instance, but the babysitter's consistent attempts to use RAB that result in the cooperation that amazes the parent.

## 158. The babysitter's bag of tricks.

A babysitter comes each time equipped with a bag with some fun things to do: a couple of frisbees and a plan for a game, a cooperative game of throwing hoops onto some stakes, some picture books, a ball and a plan for a cooperative soccer activity, a musical instrument and some songs to sing, a story to tell, a jump rope and several cooperative jumping activities, some puzzles, a map of the stars and a plan for star-gazing, a map and compass and a plan for a cooperative challenge of "find the treasure by following the map," some magic tricks, and so forth. Usually these activities require a little explanation and direction about how to do them, but when the children follow those directions, it's fun.

Analysis: The babysitter is becoming a "generalized reinforcer" by repeatedly having fun times with the children. In addition, each time the children follow the directions for how to do an activity and find that the activity is fun, there is RAB for the crucial behavior of following the babysitter's directions.

## 159. "Kindness" to the binge drinker.

A college student has a roommate who very frequently binge drinks alcohol. The student, who is conscientious and kind, exerts a great deal of effort to make sure that the roommate is safe – drives when it is not safe for the roommate to drive, makes sure the roommate doesn't pass out in the cold, guides the roommate back to the room when the roommate is too confused to get back, tries to make sure the roommate doesn't get taken advantage of by other people, wakes the roommate up to prevent oversleeping when there are important tests, etc. The binge-drinking behavior of the roommate gets more and more frequent.

Analysis: The kind and conscientious college student prevents a certain amount of PUB that would come from the environment for the drunken

191

behavior. In addition, the nurturing and caretaking behavior may be reinforcing to the roommate; if so, the student is providing RUB.

While the student may not want to let the roommate get into very dangerous situations, the student may want to consider other ways of being kind: notifying the roommate's parents about the dangerousness of the behavior, petitioning to move to a different room, insisting that the roommate get mental health services, insisting that alcohol not be kept in their room, and/or saying "No" to unreasonable requests. RUB for alcoholic behavior can be quite dangerous for the recipient of the reinforcement, and very draining for the giver.

Abraham Twerski wrote a book called: *Caution: "Kindness" Can Be Dangerous to the Alcoholic.* Part of his goal was to help people not to deliver RUB and not to prevent too many of the natural consequences that would constitute PUB – and thus not to be an enabler of alcoholism.

I tend to define the word *kindness* as doing things that help a person in the long run. With that use of the word, "not spoiling," or refusing to reinforce unwanted behavior, can be a very kind act, and that sort of kindness is good for the alcoholic.

## 160. Who can make the child stop moping?

Some college students run an after-school program for children. One of the children looks sad and curls up on a table. One of the college students goes to the child and rubs the child's back and tries to get the child to cheer up or to tell what is wrong. When this doesn't work, another college student comes to help out. Finally they get the leader of the program to come. All of them rub and pet the child. Over time, this behavior becomes more frequent, not only for this child, but for other ones as well.

Analysis: No reasonable person would say that you should never console or comfort someone who feels bad. Nonetheless, the fact remains that many children crave individual attention, many are highly reinforced by nurturing kindness, and individual attention may be hard to come by in a large group setting. It could be that the nurturing attention and rubs constitute RUB, and that the college students are inadvertently teaching the child to act morose in order to get their reinforcing attention. It could be that the answer to the question, "What's the matter?" is, "I want you to ask me what's the matter, that's what!" The fact that the behavior is going up in frequency suggests that something is reinforcing it; the fact that other students start doing it more frequently suggests that they are getting vicarious reinforcement for such behavior.

## 161. Giving a moping child space.

At another after school program run by college students, a child curls up on top of a table and looks depressed. A college student friend says, "You look kind of sad. Want to talk about it?" When the child shakes the head "No," a college student says, "That's OK; we'll give you your space." The college students leave the child alone for a while, and when the child is ready, the child joins in activities.

The next day, the same child is sitting and looking at a book. A college student friend sits beside her, and looks at the book with her. When she finishes looking at the book, the college student says, "So tell me about your life these days. What makes you happy, and what makes you unhappy?" The child is able to talk some about how life is going for her, and the college student is a good listener.

Analysis: Being a good listener to a child is a good thing, not a bad thing. The child's self-disclosure to a trustworthy older person is almost always something worth reinforcing.  But the interest and attention of the older person should reinforce the child's collaborative communication, not the child's refusal to talk. In this vignette the students non-reinforced the child's withdrawal. But later, the college student reinforced both the admirable behavior of looking at the book and the admirable behavior of chatting. If we consider the withdrawal unwanted, the college student used a combination of NUB and RAB, which is "differential reinforcement in the right direction."

## 162. I'll come out if you do what I want.

Some college students run an after school program. One of the children crawls under a table, and says that she won't come out unless a certain college student, her favorite, comes to talk to her. The favorite college student calls to her from a distance that the rule is that the students who are not under tables get worked with first. The favorite college student asks the other college students to leave the child alone. Gradually the child ventures out. When she has been out for a while, the favorite college student gives her some positive attention in the same way that she does when the child has not been under the table.

Analysis: The child is making a bid for a RUB-RUB exchange: if you'll reinforce me for extorting you, I'll reinforce you by making you feel effective. The favorite college student wisely turns down that bid, and uses NUB – non-reinforces the unwanted behavior. When the child comes out and acts normal, the favorite college student now employs RAB. The combination of NUB and RAB constitutes "differential reinforcement in the right direction." If the favorite college student had specifically given lots of positive attention to the child for coming out, she would have been reinforcing the end of a chain of behavior that was unwanted. But she attempts to avoid this trap, and if the reinforcement is not felt by the child as contingent upon refusing to come out, but contingent upon ordinary participation, the favorite college student may indeed have successfully avoided the trap.

## 163. Without monitoring, you can't tell what works.

A child sometimes hits or kicks at home. The parents want to implement a time out program. But they know that if the child is told to go to a time out room, the child will simply noncomply. So they come up with a plan that each morning, they will put 5 pieces of candy in a jar that only they have access to. Each time the child refuses to go to time out, one of the pieces of candy will be taken out of the jar. At the end of the day, the child gets whatever candy is left, plus an additional piece if there were no time outs at all.

Later, someone asks, "How is the program working?" The parent says, "There are good days and bad days, still. We did it for a while, and it seems like things got better. We've been so stressed lately that we've all kind of forgotten about it. We haven't really followed through with it. Things might have gotten worse lately – I'm not sure."

Analysis: The plan is to use time out as PUB for aggression, and to use the candy as RAB for the admirable behavior of either not needing time out or complying with time out. Alternatively, we can call the withdrawal of the candy PUB for refusing to comply with time out.

However, a main point that this vignette illustrates is that in order to use applied behavior analysis effectively, you have to keep track of how frequently the behavior in question occurs, over time. Otherwise, you can't answer the question of whether the plan you've instituted is "working" or not. An even more important point is that a program won't work unless it is actually carried out, no matter how good the plan is. Before committing to a plan, parents should ask themselves, "Do I really have the energy and the time and the organization to follow through with this?" If the answer is no, a different plan should be selected, for the time being.

## 164. Trying to punish laziness, but also punishing studenthood

A piano teacher sternly reprimands students if they have not practiced enough – and almost all of them have not. The teacher has them try playing the assigned work, points out all that is wrong with it, and shows them what they would have learned if they had practiced enough. Then the teacher grills them about what they were doing wasting time when they could have been practicing.

The piano teacher finds that most students drop out quickly, and the piano teacher's income is very low.

Analysis: One of the problems with using PUB is that admirable behavior often gets punished along with the unwanted behavior. The teacher wanted to punish the behavior of "goofing off instead of practicing." Along with it, the teacher punished the behavior of "participating in piano lessons with this teacher." As a result, the teacher got punished by loss of income.

## 165. "Nondirective" therapy, but still influential

A therapist tries very hard to be nondirective. Most of the therapist's utterances are *reflections*, or restatements of what the client has communicated. This is the therapeutic style founded by Carl Rogers. For example:

Client: I feel so fed up with my family. They're just a bunch of slackers, and they always will be. Why should I keep waiting on them hand and foot? I feel like running off to Brazil without even saying goodbye to any of them.

Therapist: Sounds like you've really had it with their not doing their share, and you really want something about this picture to change quickly.

Or:

Client: I'm finding that when I am not so irritable with them, they reciprocate, and we actually have fun together. I don't mind doing work to help people who at least speak to me with a kind tone of voice.

Therapist: Sounds like you've done some productive

thinking. If I understand you right, you've put your finger on something really important to you – that people speak to each other in a positive way. If there's a good emotional climate, you aren't so worried about how work is divided up. And you've discovered that you have some control, because how you act toward them can greatly affect that emotional climate. Do I understand correctly?

The therapist has recorded many sessions, and many clients have gotten lots better. Someone studies the recordings, and concludes that the therapist seems actually to pick what the therapist sees as the most positive, healthy parts of the client's utterances to attend to and restate. The person studying the recordings notices, in the examples above, that the first reflection was NOT:

Therapist: So leaving them permanently sounds like a good idea, and Brazil is a good place to move to, huh?

And the second reflection was NOT:

Therapist: So if I understand you right, all it takes is a little sweet talk to you and you are ready to abandon working out a fair division of labor.

Analysis: The person studying the recordings concluded that the therapist used NUB and RAB: the therapist systematically ignored the parts felt to be least wise and healthy, and reflected with tones of approval the parts felt to be most wise and healthy.

This brings out the fact that it is virtually impossible *not* to use differential reinforcement in conversations. We react in some way to everything the other person says, and we are bound to respond in more reinforcing ways to to some things the person says than to others.

Someone whose differential reinforcement is "therapeutic" has a good sense of what is healthier and wiser to think and do, and responds in a more reinforcing way to the healthier thoughts. Of course, what is healthier is debatable. Perhaps sometimes leaving one's family and running off to Brazil without saying goodbye is the wisest thing to do. If the therapist knows that the client is short of money, couldn't find a job in Brazil, doesn't know Portuguese, and doesn't even like the Samba, the therapist may feel fairly confident in not "differentially reinforcing" that option!

## 166. Good behavior game, a.k.a. class behavior game.

A teacher leads a classroom where behavior problems are the major challenge. The teacher reads the following directions about how to play the Good Behavior Game, a.k.a. the Class Behavior Game.

1. You define very clearly what the undesirable behaviors are.

2. You divide the classroom into teams, maybe 3 or 4 of them, trying to make the teams as evenly matched as possible.

3. You find some really reinforcing rewards that can be given to the successful team members.

4. You announce the game and at first you only do it for short times, like 10 to 30 minutes. You tell the students the rules and the rewards. You set a timer to mark the end of the game period.

5. Each time a team member does something disruptive, you put a mark on the blackboard by the team name.

6. At the end of the time, the reinforcers go to any or

all teams that are below a certain preset number of marks.

7. You can keep track of the scores and add them up across the whole week, and the winning teams at the end of the week get another prize.

8. If there are children who enjoy sabotaging their team's performance by purposely being disruptive, the teams are rearranged so that all these children are put on a team of their own.

9. The teacher uses interpersonal artistry to harness the competitive spirit among the teams, but at the same time reinforce more than one team if they met the desired criterion.

Analysis: Getting a mark on the board against one's team is certainly meant to be a punishing event – PUB. The disapproval of the team members is probably the main punishment. If the team as a whole can do few enough infractions, there are some really reinforcing prizes, so there is RAB.

    Some children might delight in bringing down their teammates, perhaps getting revenge on them. To prevent these kids from getting RUB, there is a prior plan to make a team composed only of any saboteurs.

The manuals for the game instruct the teacher to respond calmly to the infractions, name what they are, praise the teams that are doing well, put up the mark, and go on. If the children respond positively to the game, their good behavior reinforces the teacher for the calm response to misbehaviors rather than, for example, screaming in response to them.

Some people might complain, "Why not reinforce positive behaviors rather than just the absence of negative ones? Why not count positive behaviors?" The hope is that negative behaviors will become much less frequent than positive ones, and thus the recording of negative behaviors will be much less burdensome than trying to record every positive behavior.

## 167. Internet threats.

According to a story reported in the New York Times Magazine ("Screen Crime," by Emily Bazelon, November 30, 2014), a man wrote remarks on Facebook, addressed to his wife who had left him 5 months earlier. He said, among other things, "I'm not gonna rest until your body is a mess, soaked in blood and drying from all the little cuts." And: "If I only knew then what I know now... I would have smothered [you] with a pillow. Dumped your body off in the back seat. Dropped you off in

Toad Creek and made it look like a rape and murder."

This case made it to the U.S. Supreme Court regarding rights of free speech versus the right not to be threatened. But the reason it's of interest here is the argument the man made (and apparently his lawyers agreed to take seriously): "This is therapeutic." Talking about the loss of his wife "helps me to deal with the pain."

Analysis: There is a long-standing, incorrect, and very harmful idea that it is necessary to express hostile fantasies or wishes in order to "get them out of the system" or "work through one's anger." This has been known as the "catharsis hypothesis" – that giving expression to anger reduces anger. A great deal of research has discredited the catharsis hypothesis. A good deal of this was summarized in a book by psychologist Carol Tavris, *Anger: The Misunderstood Emotion.*

From an applied behavior analysis point of view, if having violent fantasies and wishes about his wife and communicating them to the public, including his wife, actually reduced the man's pain, then the pain-reduction is a reinforcer for the threats. And making violent threats is probably in the same "response class" as actual violence. Thus the man is probably experiencing RUB for very

205

maladaptive behavior. The idea that such behavior is "therapeutic" is a sad commentary on cultural beliefs about therapy.

Why do violent revenge fantasies or actions sometimes reduce people's pain after they have been criticized or rejected or humiliated? One theory is that people have a wish for dominance, and acts or fantasies of violence restores their position on the dominance ladder from "below" to "above" the person who they think hurt them. Disclaimer: I have not interviewed or examined the real person in the court case, and cannot say whether this applies to him (and probably couldn't say for sure even if I had).

## 168. Positive behavior diary.

A parent watches for the child's positive examples of psychological skills. The parent already tries to reinforce those examples by 1) an immediate reaction, usually of some excitement and approval; 2) telling someone else about the positive example, and 3) reviewing the positive example with the child at bedtime each night, either by narrating it or by acting it out with puppets or toy people.

The parent decides to go the extra mile with the positive examples, and to write down the examples in a "positive behavior diary." Each day the parent opens a word processing file and adds entries with the date and a little story of what the child did. The parent tries to have these stories be as concrete as possible. Thus, for example, rather than saying, "She was kind when her brother interrupted her," the parent writes, "Sarah was studying for a test. Her brother Felix interrupted her and said, 'Sarah, please come look at what I built!' She said, 'What you built! I want to see that! Let me come to a stopping point really quickly... OK! Show me!' And then she ran with him to look. It was a model of the Eiffel Tower. She said, 'Wow! You did this! How did you figure out how to put all those little pieces together? That's amazing!' After a while she said, 'I wish I could look longer, Felix. But I have to get back to studying. I have a test tomorrow! Thanks for showing me this!' And then she went straight back to work. I celebrate her kindness and her productivity!"

The parent keeps doing this, and the Positive Behavior Diary gets longer and longer. Every once in a while, the parent and the child sit down and read it together, or the parent reads it to the child at bedtime. The frequency of the positive examples rises. Years later, the children cherish the diaries their parent kept.

Analysis: The positive behavior diary is a great way

of increasing RAB. The entries demonstrate to the child that the positive examples are being noticed, and that there is a permanent record kept of them. Each time the positive examples are revisited by reading the diary, there is another reinforced fantasy rehearsal of the positive examples that are read. In addition, the child gets strong evidence for the parent's love and caring, that the parent is willing to do the work entailed in this project.

## 169. Contingent reinforcement in return for college tuition.

A college aged student has lots of free time during the summer, and is interested in learning more about physics. The student buys a very good textbook, with very clear explanations. The student tries to get around to studying the book regularly, but other things just get in the way.

The student then resumes college, and takes a course in physics that uses the same textbook. There are assignments that must be turned in, for a grade, twice a week. There are frequent tests. There are discussions, and if someone has not studied, the discussions are not fun, but otherwise they are quite enjoyable. At the end of the course the student gets a grade and credit that can be used as part of a credential. The student learns lots of physics, and enjoys doing so.

Analysis: The point of this vignette is to illustrate the point that educational institutions are not selling information – information is already available on the Internet, in books, and elsewhere. Rather, they are selling reinforcement and punishment contingencies. Grades on assignments and tests, differing amounts of enjoyment of discussion, and the credit received for the course are all versions of RAB and PUB (and sometimes, unfortunately, PAB). It could be that if schools would acknowledge more that reinforcement contingencies are what they have to supply that people have trouble furnishing on their own, they might do a better job of individualizing and maximizing the effectiveness of these contingencies.

Some individuals can supply enough internal reinforcement to keep them motivated to learn. Some can even learn better independently than at college. It will be good if higher education gains more ability to accommodate all sorts of learning styles.

## 170. The bullies enjoy the victim's protests.

Two middle-school aged kids are rather awkward and not very socially skilled. Both of them start to get taunts and insults from bullying peers at school. The first responds by giving them a blank or puzzled look and saying nothing. The second responds by protesting with great emotion: "Stop saying that! I don't like that! You have no right! Leave me alone!" The bullies gradually come to leave the first kid alone, but the taunts to the second kid increase greatly.

Analysis: The angry protests of the second kid are apparently reinforcers for the bullying behavior. If the second kid could learn to stop reinforcing the bullying, perhaps the bullying behavior would decrease. As to explaining why angry protests should be reinforcing, we can invoke either human motives for power and dominance, and/or original sin.

Comment: This is not to imply that the solution to this problem should be the responsibility of the bullied kid. The rule of law should prevail, and no child should have to endure frequent taunts at school. However, the power of school personnel to enforce civil behavior between students, if the students aren't initially inclined that way, is unfortunately considerably less than complete.

## 171. Rescue, but no thanks.

A person's car gets stuck in the snow late at night. The person calls up a family member, who is already asleep, to come and give a ride home; the plan is that the car can stay where it is until the morning. On the way home, they get into a little dispute that distracts them; the person doesn't thank the family member for getting out of bed and coming to pick the person up.

Analysis: This is classic NAB. It takes such a short time and so little effort to say thank you, but most of us human beings pass up the opportunity for RAB really often.

## 172. "I'm bad." "No, you're good."

A person makes a mistake, and comments, "I'm so stupid." A family member who wants very much for the person to have high self-esteem, contradicts this, saying, "You're not stupid at all. You're one of the smartest people around," and then gives evidence for the assertion. The person later says, "Why do I look so ugly?" In response, a family member showers the person with compliments about the person's looks. Over time, the self-criticism seems to increase in frequency.

Analysis: Compliments are usually reinforcing, and in this case the behavior they reinforce is self-critical statements. Thus there is RUB going on. The family members would do better to shower the person with compliments after the person's admirable behaviors, so as to convert RUB to RAB.

## 173. Reinforcer not delivered.

A child is promised a trip to a certain restaurant as a celebration when the child finishes a big piece of work. But when the child finally finishes, the parents are very stressed and busy, and don't have time for a trip to the restaurant. After some time has passed, they have second thoughts about wasting money on the restaurant. After still more time has passed, they figure that because of the time gradient of reinforcement, (the fact that rewards have less effect on behavior when they occur long after the behavior) it's too late for the expenditure to do any good.

Analysis: The parents set out to use RAB, but

the failure to deliver is probably disappointing enough for the child that the result is PAB instead. The moral of this story is that the time to consider whether a reinforcer is too expensive or difficult is before it is offered, not after it is earned!

## 174. Reinforcer delivered before being earned.

Parents plan with a child that when the child accumulates 20 days with overall ratings of 7 or greater, the family will celebrate by getting a new fish for the fish tank. This is highly desirable to the child.

When the child has accumulated 15 days, the parent happens to see a sale where an exceptionally desirable fish is available at a low price. The parent seizes this opportunity, and brings the fish home to celebrate a few days early.

Analysis: The phrase "contingent reinforcement" means that the reinforcer "is contingent on," or depends upon, a certain amount of a certain behavior. It describes a relationship where "If, and only if, you do X (behavior), you will get Y (reinforcer)." If the parent delivers the reinforcer without its having been fully earned, the contingent nature of the reinforcer is been undermined. The effect is that if in the future, the parent plans reinforcers contingent on certain behaviors, the child will be less likely to believe that the behavior is really necessary to get the reinforcer. Both failing to deliver and delivering prematurely undermine the contingent nature of the reinforcement.

The parent perhaps could have bought the fish but asked a friend or relative to keep it until the child earned the reinforcer.

## 175. Would feel too guilty to withhold the social event reinforcer.

A parent tells a child that he can have a play date with a friend if the child has days rated 7 out of 10 or above for a total of 5 more days. The child finds out that the friend is available 5 days from now, but not for a while after that. They make tentative plans to get together. But then the child has a very bad day that the parent can't rate as 7 or above, or anywhere close to it. After that, the child has 4 really good days. The parent can't bear to cancel the play date for something that happened 5 days ago, and the kids get together.

Analysis: The parent rightly doesn't want to provide PAB, which is what would happen if the play date were canceled. But by not sticking to the

214

deal, the parent is undermining the contingent nature of the reinforcement.

As a general rule, reinforcers which have to happen on a certain date or not at all, and reinforcers whose withholding would disappoint other people or socially embarrass the person are not the best ones to choose. But at any rate, the time to make the calculation, "Would I feel too guilty about withholding the reinforcer," is before the deal is offered.

## 176. We tried for good behavior and we got haggling.

A mom and dad start a reinforcement program, where the child gets a certain number of points for each comply, a certain number of points for each day of keeping cool (without a tantrum), and a certain number of points for time spent working. The child accumulates points toward several desirable reinforcers.

Each time the child is asked to do something, the child asks if she will get points for complying. If the answer is yes, the child asks how many points. Often the child says, "I think that this is a big job. I think it deserves more points than that." If the child has a small tantrum, and gets no points, the child says, "But I got zero points when I had a really big tantrum. This was a small one. I think I should get a few points." The parents negotiate with the child, and every once in a while the child makes a cogent enough argument that the parents give extra points. But the parents finally get so annoyed with all the haggling that they discontinue the program.

Analysis: The child is getting intermittently reinforced for haggling by getting extra points. The child is probably getting more consistently reinforced for haggling by the stimulation and attention and power gained from the haggling process. Along with the RAB the program is meant to provide, it also provides RUB – the parents apparently do not have a goal of preparing their child for an eventual career as a professional haggler of some sort.

The fact that the child is motivated to haggle is a good sign: it implies that the child is motivated for points. This is a better type of problem to have than the problem of the child who is indifferent to the reinforcers.

This problem can usually be eliminated by establishing a very clear ground rule at the beginning that the "judges' decisions are final." Attempts at haggling result in a Buddha-like smile, a monotone reminder that haggling only moves the ratings downward rather than upward, silence, or some other non-reinforcing response.

## 177. Robbing the critic of the pleasure of the power to hurt

A child, Don, says to another child, Zack, "You're such a messy person. Look at all the mess you have. You're lazy not to clean it up."

Zack says, "You've got a point there. I could work a lot harder on cleaning up."

Later, Don says, "You've got such an annoying voice."

Zack replies, "Oh, tell me more about that. How can I improve it?"

A lot later, Don says to Zack's mother, "You look really old."

Zack's mother replies, "I am really old. But you want to know something amazing? Every day I get even older!" Zack and his mom laugh at this.

They notice that over time, Don's frequency of insults goes down.

Analysis: Sometimes the motive for someone to be insulting and critical is the excitement and power that comes when the other person defends himself or herself. By responding with "agreeing with criticism," or "asking for more specific criticism," or silent curiosity, or any other response that gives the message, "I have not been wounded," the criticized person robs the critic of the feeling of power and excitement. Instead of furnishing RUB, the person furnishes NUB.

## 178. This time the insult gets punished

An adolescent attends a private school. He gets angry and calls the teacher an obscene and insulting name, in the middle of class. He looks to notice the shocked or amused or startled reactions of his classmates. This is the second time he has done this; he had received a severe warning the first time; he is expelled from the school.

The adolescent's parent says, "I think the teacher should have just ignored it. He was just trying to get a reaction."

Analysis: In this vignette, the teacher's reaction is not the only source of reinforcement – the fame, notoriety, and attention received from peers is probably much stronger RUB. Plus, the teacher and the school personnel are rightly concerned about the vicarious message the other students get if the student is allowed to use obscene insults with impunity. The expulsion constitutes PUB if the student liked the school, and RUB if he hated it. But what the school officials are most interested in is the vicarious PUB and its impact on the other students.

## 179. Insanity or mental deficiency defense

A person committed a serious crime. The person acts as his own lawyer. He shows up at the trial in a Superman outfit, attempts to call a famous female rock star as a witness, and says crazy-sounding things from start to finish. He is found not guilty by reason of insanity. Instead of execution, he gets treatment at a hospital.

Analysis: The escape from execution into a fairly humane hospital was certainly a powerful reinforcer for the illness behavior. Whether the person also had a severe illness that gives reason for irrational behavior is impossible to say from this vignette. It is undeniably true that some people have successfully faked mental illness in order to escape aversive consequences. Probably many more have unconsciously come up with symptoms in order to escape aversive circumstances, not even being aware of what they are doing. The pity that society has toward people who can't help what they do certainly creates as a side effect a certain amount of RUB for becoming incapacitated.

## 180. Anxiety gets extension on work

A student is in treatment for anxiety. The student is behind in academic work. The student's clinician writes a letter which allows the person to get an extension for work. Another student who has a "partying addiction disorder" does not get an extension.

Analysis: Freud called benefits such as extensions on academic work "secondary gain for illness." Applied behavior analysts would call such benefits reinforcers. Sometimes such medical excuses have a net positive effect on the person being excused, and sometimes the reinforcing effect is harmful. Predicting whether disability excuses will be helpful or harmful is not easy.

## 181. Out of control child escapes punishment

Child 1 defies a parent's command, and gets screen time withdrawn for a day as a punishment. Child 2, the sibling, gets a command from a parent, starts screaming, throwing things, dumping things over, hitting people, and screaming even louder when anyone speaks to him. Finally the episode ends, and Child 2 goes to sleep. The parents don't impose a punishment for this for two reasons: first, the child seemed not able to control the behavior, and second, they don't want to precipitate another episode by the punishment.

Analysis: The movement from "deserving punishment" status to "free of punishment" status is a reinforcer, which is RUB for 1) being out of control and 2) having very aversive behaviors. The parents' attempts to exert reasonable control over the child have been punished, and if they "walk on eggshells" in response, the power the child gains also probably reinforces the tantrum behavior.

People sometimes have a hard time believing that super loud and aggressive behavior could be influenced by consequences. But there's lots of evidence that rages are subject to reinforcement control.

## 182. Reading in an annoying voice during tutoring

A tutor and a child take turns reading to each other. The child starts reading in a very annoying voice. The tutor asks the child to stop, and the child stops for a while, then starts back. This happens several times. Then the tutor stops responding to the annoying voice. Eventually the child too finds it annoying, and stops using it.

Analysis: It sounds as if NUB worked to decrease the frequency of the behavior. The requests to stop may have been RUB.

## 183. Learning not to self-punish verbally

Someone pursues various goals, but when the person makes the slightest mistake, she is in the habit of saying things to herself, very often, such as, "Oh, I did something stupid!" and "Why can't I do anything right?" and "I looked like an idiot then!" The person gets depressed.

The person goes to a cognitive therapist who teaches her to substitute other types of thoughts, such as, "What can I learn from that mistake?... Hooray, I learned something that will help me." and "What are my options now? ... Hooray, I think I made a good choice." and "This is such a trivial thing that I don't want to punish myself over this. My goal is to keep on having fun!" and "Hooray, I've accomplished something," The person feels lots better.

Analysis: Frequent uncontrollable punishment tends to be depressing. This is especially true when the punishment occurs contingent upon trying to achieve goals. Self-delivered verbal punishment disrupts the effort-payoff connection just as externally delivered punishment does.

When the person shuts off much of the self-punishment and starts using some self-reinforcement, the effort-payoff connection is restored.

The "before treatment" thoughts were classified as getting down on herself, whereas the "after treatment" thoughts were examples of learning from the experience, listing options and choosing, goal-setting, not getting down on oneself, and celebrating one's own choice.

## 184. The case of the subdued greeting

Two people greet each other. "Hey," says the first, in a low, grunt-like, barely audible sound.

"Hunh," says the other, in the same tone.

A second pair exchange greetings. "Hey, look who's here, gimme five! Long time no see!" says the first, in very animated tones.

"Hey there! Good to see you, buddy! How in the world have you been doing!" says the second of pair 2.

Analysis: It certainly appears that the members of the second pair are reinforcing each other's socializing quite a bit more than the first pair.

The members of the first pair are pretty much non-reinforcing the start of socialization – it sounds like NAB. Someone may say, "In the culture of the first pair, the subdued greeting ritual is just as reinforcing." It appears to me, however, that enthusiasm and interest and excitement are expressed similarly across many cultures. Tones of voice seem to have similar meanings, for example, no matter what language people speak. My guess is that enthusiastic greetings usually are more reinforcing.

If someone were to invent a meter that accurately measured the activity in the "pleasure centers" of the brain, this device might be quite a boon in applied behavior analysis, particularly if one quick reading could answer the fundamental question, "What is the effect of this consequence upon the long-term frequency of the behavior?" We will not hold our breaths while waiting for such an invention!

## 185. Reinforcing resolution-breaking during weight loss attempt

Someone is trying to lose weight. The person thinks, "Today I'm going to eat only at meals, with nothing between." But the person walks into the kitchen while a family member is having something to eat, and it looks so good that the person thinks, "I can't pass this up," and has a pretty big snack. The person says, "I'll make up for this by having a very small supper." But when suppertime comes, the food tastes so good that the person thinks, "Tomorrow I'll pace myself better," and has a very large supper.

Analysis: The pleasure of food of course reinforces eating. But here it's reinforcing something else in addition: the breaking of resolutions. Thinking, "I know I resolved to do this, but I'm just not strong enough to do it now," gets reinforced by food. Resolution-breaking behavior is just what is not wanted by someone who is trying to lose weight. So food becomes RUB.

## 186. Reinforcing resolution-keeping during weight loss attempt

Someone who is trying to lose weight decides to put the biggest emphasis on resolution-keeping behavior. The person, before each meal, resolves to eat a certain amount of food and then to stop, and not eat until the next meal. The person writes down what the resolution is, listing each menu item and amount. When the person starts the meal, the person remembers to think, "Hooray for me for not eating since the previous meal!" At the end of the meal, the person thinks, "Yay, I stopped when I had resolved to stop!"

Analysis: When using self-discipline, it's important to get out of the sin-guilt-repentance-sin cycle. The first order of business is to establish the habit of following one's own resolutions. The self-talk that the person models in this vignette constitutes crucial RAB for resolution-keeping behavior.

Benjamin Franklin often repeated the following words as part of a prayer he composed: "Increase in me that wisdom which discovers my truest Interests; strengthen my resolutions to perform what that wisdom dictates."

Our weight-watcher discovers that there is a golden mean for resolutions: they should be challenging enough that weight loss proceeds, but no so challenging that resolution-keeping becomes improbable.

## 187. Making computer chess a contingent reinforcer

A person finds herself wasting lots of time playing chess against the computer. She infers that because this activity is freely chosen so often, it is a powerful reinforcer. She decides to harness its reinforcing power to help her do some self-discipline requiring task. She needs to spend more time organizing: getting papers and things and computer files put into their places, keeping track of tasks, arranging to do items in order of priority, and so forth. She decides to allow herself one game of chess for each hour that she spends organizing. She can save up and play several games at one sitting if she likes.

She finds that this arrangement make both the organizing and the chess more fun.

Analysis: Deliberately giving yourself reinforcers only when you've earned them by some desirable behavior is a part of what's called self-management, self-reinforcement, or self-administered consequences. In this case the organizing becomes more enjoyable because it's reinforced; the chess becomes more enjoyable because of relative deprivation and possibly also because the person now doesn't feel guilty about it. Also, the very act of setting something up as a contingent reinforcer may make it more desirable.

The major challenge in self-management lies in not stealing the reinforcers before they are earned. I recommend a lot of congratulatory self-talk as reinforcement for this ongoing achievement of self-discipline.

Many of the activities and indulgences we call "vices" could be used as contingent reinforcers in self-management programs, with the big provisos that the person indulges in the vice/reinforcer only in rationed, measured amounts, and only when the reinforcer has been earned.

## 188. The effort-payoff connection for zoo animals

Zoo animals often get "free reinforcement." They are fed regularly without having to do anything to get the food. They don't have to protect themselves or escape from predators. They don't have to scour the environment for suitable territory. It's not too hot or too cold. Would we think that in such an environment where they get everything they need without having to lift a paw for it, they would be happy?

It turns out that there are ways of getting some pretty good clues about whether certain animals are happy. Stereotyped movements (such as pacing back and forth), not wanting to reproduce, being aggressive, having high levels of stress hormones, premature death, and so forth can be clues that we have an unhappy animal.

When animals work for their food, being

trained to obtain it by doing any of a wide range of behaviors, they seem to be much happier than when they are in conditions of "free reinforcement."

Analysis: Sometimes we think of contingent reinforcement as a way of increasing the frequency of a certain desirable behavior. But sometimes it's the contingent relationship itself that's important, not the particular behavior that is being reinforced. When an animal works to earn its rewards, there is some control over reinforcers, and this appears to be very important for almost all animals, including humans. I refer to this control as the effort-payoff connection.

You can read more about the effort-payoff connection for captive animals in an article called "Positive Reinforcement Training as an Enrichment Strategy" by Gail Laule and Tim Desmond, available on the Internet at http://activeenvironments.org/pdf/Trng_Enrich_Eeconf.pdf.

## 189. Why teach misbehaving children to do chores?

In the parent training program pioneered by Dr. Gerald Patterson, families came for help with children who were disobedient, disrespectful, aggressive, or hostile. The program usually included training children to perform household chores in exchange for reinforcers.

A young clinician raises the question, "Why is there such an emphasis on chores? The families did not come because they had problems with dishes not getting washed, or trash not being taken out, or laundry not being put away. It seems like this program is diverting attention from the really important targets for improvement."

Analysis: As the young clinician became a slightly less young clinician, answers became apparent. First, empirically, the children seemed to get better when they were reinforced for doing chores. Second, chores are an easily measurable positive behavior that can be used to create an effort-payoff connection for the child, where the parent is the source of each reinforcer. Third, chores have an inherent value that does not go away once the child becomes "normal" – that is, you would reinforce someone for "going a day without a tantrum" only if the child has had tantrums frequently, but you would reinforce someone for washing dishes as long as there are dishes to clean.

Lots of positive reinforcement for help with chores appears to have positive effects on children, just as working for reinforcement has with zoo animals! The effort-payoff connection is key to well-being.

## 190. Confucius liked differential reinforcement.

The following is from the *Analects of Confucius*, as quoted by Joseph Teluskin in *Uncommon Sense: The World's Fullest Compendium of Wisdom*.

"Someone asked Confucius, 'What do you think of repaying evil with kindness?'

Confucius replied, 'Then what are you going to repay kindness with? Repay kindness with kindness but repay evil with justice.'"

This seemingly contrasts with a Christian exhortation: "Bless them that curse you, do good to them that hate you, and pray for them who despitefully use you, and persecute you." (Matthew 5:44).

Analysis: I believe that the language of reinforcement helps, when deciding how to deal with bad behavior. Suppose Johnny hits Ms. Smith, and Ms. Smith responds by hugging Johnny and telling him she loves him. Suppose that her response reinforces Johnny's hitting, and he hits more often.

Is Ms. Smith being kind to Johnny? I would say no, if kindness means doing things that are in the person's long-term best interest. By using RUB, she is doing something harmful to him. If by providing a humane consequence that Johnny doesn't especially like, Ms. Smith can teach Johnny not to hit, she is doing something much more kind for him.

Thus what Confucius called "justice" may also be identical to "kindness!"

Suppose that Franco curses at his parent. The reinforcer he happens to be looking for is a demonstration of his power to provoke an angry and defensive response. But instead, his parent looks to the sky, and says, "May the day come when my beloved son grows into such wisdom and maturity that he can always speak with dignity and respect." Suppose that this behavior fails to reinforce Franco's cursing, and the rate of his unwanted behavior falls. Now the parent has repaid "evil" with "kindness," and the result is positive. The parent has used NUB and has also vaguely vicariously reinforced examples of values; believing in values is an "establishing operation" for the child's finding good behavior reinforcing.

In my opinion, the kindest way to respond to bad behavior is to pick the most humane consequences (and other methods of influence) that will effectively teach that particular person to do good behavior instead. I wish I could hear whether the ancient sages would agree; my guess is that they would.

## 191. Behaviorism at a school for youth, part 1.

At a school for teenaged boys with behavior problems, the staff try a system where the boys get brief time-outs in a seclusion room for aggression. Those who are kind, compliant, and not aggressive get points for every time period with such behavior, and the points can be used to buy certain items from a store.

The incidence of aggression does not fall. In fact, it rises.

One of the staff members chats with one of the teenagers about the system. The youth says, "Anybody that never got time outs for hitting would be branded a wimp and a wuss. People respect you more if you get more time outs. And anybody who would let himself be bought off by little pieces of junk would never hear the end of it from the other guys." Conversations with other students confirm these ideas.

Analysis: The time-outs, which were meant to be PUB, turn out to be RUB because of the way the peer group sees them as a sign of toughness. And the points and prizes, which were meant to be RAB, turn out to be PAB, because the peer group would punish those who joined in the game of earning them. When a program reinforces unwanted behavior and punishes admirable behavior, it's time to say: 1) "Oops" and 2) "Back to the drawing board."

## 192. Behaviorism at a school for youth, part 2.

A new program director takes over at school for teenaged boys with behavior problems. This director is into physical fitness, and impresses the boys both with what he can do, and his physique. He does away with the point program. He tells the boys stories about American Indians and their culture, while taking them on trips to the woods. He impresses upon them the importance of the value that you don't hurt members of your own tribe. He has regular councils, in which the group members commend those behaviors of others that make the tribe better, and discuss what to do about those behaviors that make the tribe worse. The tribe's values are repeated often, in rituals the boys do not make fun of. Competitions are engineered, where the whole tribe of students is called upon to try to get into the upper percentiles of performance on tasks, relative to what other groups elsewhere have done.

The rate of aggression falls. Seclusion and restraint need to be used much less often than before.

Staff members conclude from these events that "Behaviorism doesn't work, but this works."

Analysis: Events like this don't disprove any of the tenets of applied behavior analysis, or behaviorism. It still remains true that positive reinforcement and non-reinforcement and punishment "work." Events like this prove that in order to be an effective behaviorist, you have to see whether the consequences that you think will increase or decrease the rates of behavior really do so! If the consequences you are using don't do what you want them to, you don't just keep applying them. The consequences that work for some people, and some groups, do not work for others.

The new program director engineered a set of reinforcing and punishing consequences, largely delivered by the peer group. What is reinforcing and what is punishing depends heavily upon the meaning given to those events. The "establishing operations" that create meaning for events can be very subtle and complex.

## 193. The child decides against a point plan.

Parents go to a behavior specialist and devise a plan where each day, the child will get a behavior rating ranging from 0 to 10. The child earns various reinforcers or has them withheld depending on the ratings.

The child at first is excited about the plan, and earns some reinforcers. But the first time that the child fails to earn the desired rating, the child screams, "I don't want this stupid point program any more!" and rips to shreds the paper where the records were kept.

The parents stop the program and come back to the behavior specialist and say, "It didn't work, he rejected the plan."

Analysis: The parents gave the child way too much power. The plan was set up because the child wasn't cooperative and compliant enough. Doesn't it seem unwise to make the program's existence depend on the child's consistent enthusiasm about it? Would the parents be so quick to capitulate if the child said, "I don't want to learn any of this stupid school stuff, ever again!" The child's tantrum is reinforced by his getting more power than is good for him; he's getting RUB.

What the parents should do is to keep a backup copy of the ratings that the child cannot destroy. If the child goes on strike against the program, that's his right; he just goes without reinforcers. If he rips up the public chart, he doesn't find out his rating without asking. When he gets good ratings, the reinforcers come. He gets RAB and NUB whether he votes for the program or not.

## 194. Anger control through thought rehearsal with hypothetical provocations.

Someone has a big problem with anger outbursts. A therapist teaches the person to do the *four-thought exercise* with hypothetical provocations. In the four-thought exercise, you figure out a way to apply each of the following four types of thoughts to the situation in question: 1) not awfulizing, 2) goal-setting, 3) listing options and choosing, and 4) celebrating your own choice. For example, the provocation is that someone breaks in front of someone else in line. The person might rehearse the four thoughts like this: 1) This is not a big deal; we'll all get there eventually anyway. 2) My goal is to stay cool and enjoy the evening, and my job description does not include teaching that person a lesson. 3) I could say, "Excuse me, the line forms at the rear," or I could say, "Are you wanting to get in front of me in the line?" or I could just forget about it and go back to my conversation with my friend. I'm choosing the last one. 4) Hooray, I'm glad I stayed cool and didn't let this bother me!

The person does the four-thought exercise with several hundred provocations from a standard list, and the person adds more situations to the list. Such drill and practice results in major improvement in the person's anger control skills. The result is dramatic reduction of screaming, hostile words, and physical aggression!

Analysis: Reinforced practice of admirable patterns, or RAB, is revered continually in this book. In this example the admirable thought patterns are carried out in fantasy rehearsal, and much of the reinforcement is self-delivered, in the form of celebratory thoughts.

In this example, both the behaviors being reinforced in the practice sessions, and the reinforcers themselves, are thoughts rather than overt visible behaviors. The ideas of behaviorism can fit very nicely into a rubric where thoughts reinforce other thoughts, with the eventual result of influencing more overt behaviors.

## 195. Nagging cessation as negative reinforcer for homework?

A mom repeatedly suggests that her son start his homework, in tones of voice that are anxious, demanding, worried, angry, but definitely not cheerful. This strategy doesn't work. The son tells someone else, "If I went and started it when she nags at me, that would just tell her to nag more often. I feel obligated *not* to start it then." But his strategy to try to get her not to nag doesn't work either.

Analysis: I mentioned earlier the "ignore good behavior and punish bad behavior" as a default strategy for human beings. But there's another default strategy that seems built into our brains just as strongly: nag someone to do something until the person does it. The cessation of the nagging is a negative reinforcer; the reinforcer for the behavior is that the nagging ceases.

The problem is that this strategy runs up against the "punish unwanted behavior" module. The son, in this case, wants to punish, or at least not reward, his mom for the nagging, because to him it is unwanted behavior. For him to salute and say, "Yes, mom," and to rush off to do his homework would be to reinforce her unwanted behavior. But

239

since he gets around to doing the homework sooner or later, usually, his mom is intermittently reinforced. And she gets lots of practice with the reminders, just as he gets lots of practice with ignoring them.

## 196. New deal between mom and son on homework.

The mother and son of the previous vignette have several conversations about how the mom can best help with motivating homework. They consider the option of the mom's dropping out of the homework-motivation business altogether, but the son decides that he is not quite ready for that. They agree that the son will set an alarm for a certain time. The mom will not mention homework before then. If the son gets started at that time or before, the mom will congratulate the son for getting going. When the son finishes the homework, they will celebrate together. If the son lets the time pass without getting started, the mom will try to remember to nag.

Analysis: The son is able to avoid the noxious nagging altogether by starting the homework on time. The mom gets to practice some positive reinforcement (congratulating and celebrating) instead of negative reinforcement, which will probably be much more fun for her. If the son procrastinates too long, the mom's nagging is at least something that the son has agreed to as part of the deal. He no longer has any rational reason not to reinforce it, because she is only living up to her part of the bargain.

# Index